Department of Health & Social Security

AIDS and Drug Misuse Part 1

Report by the Advisory Council on the Misuse of Drugs

London: Her Majesty's Stationery Office

ISBN 0 11 321134 1

Contents

Overview

Introduction

Chapter

Annexes

Advisory Council on the Misuse of Drugs

Overview

1 This is our first report on the implications of AIDS and HIV for services for drug misusers. It concentrates on measures which can be taken to tackle the spread of HIV through injecting drug misuse. Except in some parts of Scotland, the prevalence of HIV amongst injecting drug misusers appears to be low in the UK. But the speed with which the virus can spread in this way has been dramatically illustrated in Edinburgh and elsewhere. The opportunity to take preventive action must be seized now if the tragedy of Edinburgh is not to be repeated throughout the UK.

2 The report's first conclusion is that **HIV is a greater threat to public and individual health than drug misuse.** The first goal of work with drug misusers must therefore be to prevent them from acquiring or transmitting the virus. In some cases this will be achieved through abstinence. In others, abstinence will not be achievable for the time being and efforts will have to focus on risk-reduction. Abstinence remains the ultimate goal but efforts to bring it about in individual cases must not jeopardize any reduction in HIV risk behaviour which has already been achieved.

3 The most effective way of educating drug misusers about HIV, and changing their behaviour so as to minimise the risks, involves first bringing them into contact with a helping agency. At present, only a small minority of drug misusers are in touch with such services. The report discusses how larger numbers can be brought into contact with services. It concludes that community-based services for drug misusers provide the best opportunity and that considerable development and expansion is needed to ensure that accessible and attractive services are available throughout the country. It makes practical suggestions about ways in which these, and other services should attract more drug misusers. The role of general practitioners and other generic professions is also emphasised and suggestions are made to promote greater GP involvement with drug misusers. The need for specialist psychiatric services to back up these front-line services, providing help and support and accepting referrals in difficult cases, is highlighted.

Without this support, the ability of front-line services to make contact with more drug misusers and help them move away from HIV risk behaviour is seriously impaired.

4 Having established contact with drug misusers the next step is to educate them about HIV and how to avoid acquiring or transmitting it. The report recommends that all services for drug misusers should give practical and explicit advice on risk-reduction. This advice must recognise that some will carry on misusing drugs, by injection in some cases. It must also cover sexual transmission. If education is to succeed it is essential that drug misusers who cannot be persuaded to stop injecting should have access to sterile needles and syringes. The report considers this issue in some depth and concludes that a combination of syringe exchange schemes and over-the-counter sales from community pharmacies offers the best solution.

5 The role of prescribing in attracting drug misusers to services and helping them move away from HIV risk behaviour is discussed. The report concludes that prescribing is one of a number of tools which can help achieve this in some cases but stresses that it is not a panacea. It emphasises the need for treatment to be tailored to the individual drug misuser if it is to be effective in inducing a change away from HIV risk behaviour. This means that a full range of treatment options must be available in each district so that those providing services to drug misusers can select the most appropriate treatment package in each case.

6 The report considers the use of HIV antibody testing of drug misusers. The policy of testing individual clients only with informed consent is endorsed and the report urges that very full pre- and post-test counselling should be provided. The need for intensive efforts to achieve behaviour change with seropositive drug misusers is emphasised.

7 The measures recommended should enable services to make contact with a much larger proportion of drug misusers and work with them to change their behaviour. However, many drug misusers will remain 'hidden'; for them there will be a continued need for national and local education and publicity about HIV and how to avoid it.

8 The report looks at the special problems posed by the link between HIV and drug misuse in prisons and recommends urgent action to improve prisoners' education about HIV and AIDS. It stresses the importance of identifying drug misusers when they enter prison and seizing the opportu-

nity presented to educate them away from HIV risk practices and, where possible, towards sustained behaviour change.

9 Although the report covers the UK as a whole, special mention is made of the situation in Scotland which is a cause of grave concern. Prevalence of HIV amongst injecting drug users is high, particularly in the East where, in those tested, seroprevalence rates of around 50 per cent have been reported. Yet services north of the border are ill-equipped to play an effective role in combating the spread of the virus. The lack of psychiatric input to drug services and the lack of treatment options are worrying. So too is the continued shortage of injecting equipment in places and the lack of access to already overstretched counselling and advice services. Additional recommendations are made for immediate action in Scotland.

10 The measures recommended have not been costed in detail but it is clear that a substantial increase in funding for services for drug misusers will be needed. Investing now in these measures to prevent the spread of HIV will bring much greater future savings and benefits in both human and financial terms.

Introduction

The AIDS and Drug Misuse Working Group

1 The Advisory Council on the Misuse of Drugs at its meeting in May 1987 discussed the problem of the spread of HIV virus and AIDS among injecting drug misusers. It agreed that a Working Group should be set up as a matter of urgency to consider the implications of HIV and AIDS for drug misuse services and to make recommendations on how the problem should be tackled. The establishment of a Working Group was welcomed by Ministers, who agreed to provide the necessary Secretarial and other support.

2 The Working Group's Membership and Terms of Reference are at Annex A. Although the Group's remit covers all the implications of AIDS and HIV for drug misuse services, the Group decided to concentrate initially on measures which could be taken to stem the spread of the virus through injecting drug misuse.

3 Over the last four months the Group has taken oral evidence from some 30 witnesses with expertise in the drug misuse and AIDS fields. It has also received written evidence from some 40 further individuals and bodies. Annex B gives an indication of the range of individuals and bodies from whom evidence has been received. In addition the Group has studied a number of relevant research papers and summaries.

Scope of this First Report

4 This first report is concerned with measures to combat the spread of the virus. Wider aspects of the problem, particularly the management of drug users who are infected with the virus and those who have AIDS, will be covered in our second report.

5

5 This work covers the UK as a whole and the conclusions and recommendations should be taken to apply to all parts of the UK except where otherwise stated. We make some additional recommendations for Scotland in Chapter 7 and make some brief comments particular to Wales and Northern Ireland in Annex F. Throughout the report we have, for convenience, described services in English terms (e.g. Health Regions and Districts); for Scotland, Wales and Northern Ireland the relevant equivalent terms should be read.

Policy Background – AIDS, HIV and Injecting Drug Misuse

6 The Acquired Immune Deficiency Syndrome (AIDS) is a new and deadly condition caused by a virus known as the Human Immunodeficiency Virus (HIV). The first reported cases of AIDS in homosexual men and drug misusers occurred in the USA in 1981. Since then, the disease has spread rapidly. There have now been some 60,000 reported cases worldwide, including 1227 (by December 1987) in the United Kingdom. The World Health Organisation estimates that, throughout the world, there are 5–10 million people infected with HIV, and that in the next five years between $\frac{1}{2}$ million and 3 million deaths can be expected.

7 The virus – HIV – is found in semen, blood and some other body fluids and can be transmitted through transfer of these fluids. The overwhelming epidemiological evidence is that the main methods of transmission are:

- sexual intercourse (both heterosexual and homosexual);
- injecting drug misuse using contaminated needles and syringes and other equipment;
- medical use of infected blood and blood products;
- in utero infection of the unborn babies of infected mothers.

8 Injecting drug misuse using contaminated equipment has been identified as the method of transmission of the virus in 16 per cent of the known cases of infection in the UK as a whole. In Scotland, Italy and Spain, it accounts for over half of all known cases of infection with HIV. At present, in many parts of the USA and Europe, it is also the major way in which the virus is introduced into the heterosexual population.

9 Drug misuse is an illicit activity and drug misusers can be hard to make contact with. Persuading them to change their behaviour can be very difficult. Yet it is essential to do so if the spread of HIV is to be contained.

6

10 As part of its strategy to tackle AIDS the UK Government introduced three measures in 1987 aimed specifically at combating the spread of the virus through injecting drug misuse:

– first, the launch of a new AIDS and drug misuse publicity campaign designed to highlight to drug misusers the dangers of injecting, and particularly of sharing equipment. A complementary campaign aimed at discouraging drug misuse was run in parallel;
– second, the provision of extra resources to help drug misuse services play a growing role in the fight against AIDS; and
– third, the establishment of 15 pilot schemes where injecting drug misusers can exchange used needles and syringes for clean equipment. These schemes are being evaluated to help assess their effectiveness.

11 It was against this background that the Working Group began its work.

1 Background

Nature of HIV infection

1.1 We begin our report with a brief description of the nature of HIV infection. First, three points about the duration of infection and its implications:

a. on theoretical grounds, infection will be lifelong;
b. on current understanding, treatment at present and in the immediate future will at best be likely only to contain rather than eradicate infection;
c. future vaccines, if ever available, will not be available in a public health role until the mid 1990s at the earliest.

Therefore infection is, apparently, irreversible and primary preventive efforts are of supreme importance. For the forseeable future, this infection will only be contained if educational efforts are successful and risk behaviour is significantly modified.

1.2 Since infection is lifelong, the proportion of infected patients who develop AIDS or other life threatening diseases, may not be determined for several decades. Homosexual men are the most studied population; various cohort studies have shown that rates of 8 to 10 per cent per year, after 3 years, will progress to AIDS so that by 5 years 30 to 35 per cent have developed AIDS. Some studies have shown that given time the vast majority of patients will show deterioration in their immune system. The rate of progression in injecting drug misusers is likely to be at least as great as in homosexuals.

1.3 In view of the variation in rates of progression, there is much scientific interest in the role of various co-factors which may either induce or hasten the development of AIDS. Current research suggests that exposure to other infectious agents may reactivate HIV in infected cells leading to increased

9

viral production, dissemination and progression. Amongst additional suggested co-factors are continued injecting drug misuse, chronic anxiety and depression, and pregnancy (although there is conflicting evidence on this). If validated, all of these co-factors are relevant to the drug misuse problem. Of particular potential importance is work in New York amongst HIV positive drug misusers which indicates that continued non-sterile injection with impure street drugs leads to deterioration in immune status (as measured by numbers of helper T cells – those white blood cells specifically infected by HIV and involved in defence against some infections), compared to a control group of methadone-treated, infected users. Furthermore other evidence is emerging that further deterioration in immune status is associated with increased viral load (as detected in HIV antigen testing) and enhanced infectivity by injecting and sexual activity. Other work has shown that there appears to be an increased rate of transmission to the heterosexual partners of haemophiliacs whose disease had progressed to the stage that they had a marked reduction in their helper T cells. Therefore management which reduces the use of injected street drugs will have a most important role in the context of public health as well as individual health.

1.4 The spectrum of HIV diseases continues to increase, as is recognised in the new Centers for Disease Control (Atlanta) classification scheme. This is reflected in the continued expansion of the surveillance criteria for the diagnosis of AIDS. Nevertheless, it is possible that significant numbers of deaths will occur in seropositive injecting drug misusers due to conditions such as bacterial pneumonia and septicaemia which would not satisfy present criteria of AIDS, but are related to their HIV infection. HIV disease may also manifest through mechanisms other than immunosuppression. The most important examples of this are the direct neurological effects of HIV especially dementia. Dementia is a well recognised complication in AIDS and compounds the problems of management of injecting drug misusers with HIV related disease.

1.5 Currently there are increasing numbers of sick HIV positive patients undergoing long term therapy with Zidovudine (AZT, 'Retrovir'). This is a toxic, costly drug which makes major demands on patient compliance. It would appear to have a palliative role in serious HIV disease, in improving the quality of life over the short term in those who can tolerate it. In seropositive patients the therapeutic benefit of long term therapy has yet to be determined. The introduction of other less toxic therapies may alter this position, as might evidence that anti-retroviral therapy would reduce infectivity by any of the modes of transmission.

Spread of HIV and AIDS through Drug Misuse

1.6 We have noted that HIV can be passed between injecting drug misusers who share needles, syringes or other equipment which have become contaminated with infected blood. This is a major route of transmission of the virus and in some European countries the majority of cases of AIDS (Italy and Spain) or HIV infection (Scotland) have occurred through the use of contaminated injecting equipment.

1.7 In the UK, by the end of December 1987, 19 out of 1227 cases of AIDS were attributed to shared injecting practice among drug misusers. Of some 8000 people in the UK who have been found to be seropositive, almost 1300 have been injecting drug misusers. It is likely that these may represent only a small proportion of the total infected. Within these totals, Scotland accounts for just over 1300 antibody positive reports of which some 750 arise from injecting drug misuse. Some local studies in Edinburgh have found HIV seroprevalence levels of around 50 per cent amongst injecting drug users. Conversely, some small scale studies in a number of English cities have suggested seroprevalence rates of between nil and 10 per cent. These regional and local variations are mirrored in other parts of the world. In the United States, for example, seroprevalence amongst injecting drug users is estimated to range from 50 per cent to 70 per cent in New York to under 2 per cent in some other States. The reasons for such variations are not fully understood, but include the date of introduction of the virus into the local drug misusing population, and the extent of sharing of equipment.

1.8 In the UK, as in many other countries, injecting drug misuse has so far been the route of acquisition of HIV for the majority of infected women, most of whom are of child-bearing age (the vast majority in Scotland). And infected women are now giving birth to children in significant numbers. At the time of writing some 80 babies with antibodies to HIV in their blood have been born in the UK to antibody positive mothers. Whilst the presence of antibodies in a baby's blood at birth is not an accurate guide to infection, many of these children have developed, or are likely to develop, the infection and several have already died of AIDS.

1.9 Infected drug misusers can transmit HIV sexually as well as by sharing injecting equipment. Since the vast majority of drug misusers in the UK are thought to be heterosexual, sexual transmission will be an important route from them into the general heterosexual population. In one study in New York, where the virus is well established amongst injecting drug misusers, injecting drug misusers were thought to have been the source of the virus in

87 per cent of cases in which heterosexual activity was believed to be the mode of transmission.

1.10 Disturbing as the UK figures are, they do suggest that outside a small number of locations (notably Edinburgh) the virus may not yet be well established in the drug injecting community. This means that vigorous preventive measures taken now stand a good chance of stemming the spread of the virus. But the need for immediate action cannot be overstressed. The experience of Edinburgh, where the prevalence of HIV amongst injecting drug users rose to around 50 per cent within 2 years of the first seropositive sample, illustrates how rapidly the virus can spread. And the American experience – where in New York alone by the beginning of 1987, there were 3000 cases of AIDS amongst heterosexual injecting drug misusers – illustrates the potential scale of the disaster if we fail to act effectively. In the USA as a whole, a quarter of the 50,000 cases of AIDS have occurred in drug misusers, a minority of whom have also had homosexual risk activity. In Europe the proportion of cases of AIDS which has occurred in drug misusers has risen from 2 per cent in 1984 to 17 per cent in 1987 with much higher trends in some countries and cities. The future scale of the American problem has been dramatically underlined by the Coolfont Conference of AIDS experts in 1986. This group issues projections that by 1991, 270,000 cases of AIDS will have occurred in the United States. It is likely that 50,000 to 80,000 cases will have occurred in drug users and that there will be about 7000 cases due to heterosexual transmission and 3000 due to foetal transmission.

Other Viruses

1.11 There are now known to be at least 2 members of the human immunodeficiency virus family, HIV-1 (the cause of most disease in the epidemic so far) and HIV-2. The latter virus appears to cause disease of similar severity but is at present only known to be prevalent in a few West African countries. However, occasional cases are being found elsewhere. Dual infection may occur. Continued vigilance will be necessary to detect whether HIV-2, or any subsequently described HIV variants, are entering the injecting drug misuse population. Fortunately, measures to prevent the spread of HIV-1 will work in the same way with HIV-2. In addition there are other known (and probably unknown) viruses whose spread will also be reduced by the measures we are advocating. These viruses include HTLV-1 (human T cell lymphotropic virus), HTLV-2, and a variety of hepatitis viruses including hepatitis B, non-A non-B virus and delta agent.

Interaction of these viruses with each other may cause a variety of clinical outcomes but all are potentially important.

Pattern and Prevalence of Drug Misuse

1.12 In order to devise effective measures to counter the spread of HIV, and other viruses, through injecting drug misuse it is necessary to have some understanding of the pattern and scale of drug misuse. The illicit and hidden nature of the activity means it is impossible to obtain a completely accurate picture, or indeed to be certain about the accuracy of any picture. However, information about drug misusers who seek help from services, together with information on arrests and seizures, can be used in conjunction with research findings to gain some impressions about the scale and nature of drug misuse. The limitations of our information base, and ways of improving it, are discussed in Chapter 8. For the present, we concentrate on what information is available.

1.13 Doctors are statutorily required to notify in confidence the Chief Medical Officer at the Home Office when they attend a patient whom they suspect or believe to be addicted to certain controlled drugs (princip.·lly various opioids and cocaine). In 1986 the total number of drug misusers notified in this way (including new and re-notifications and those receiving treatment at the beginning of the year) was nearly 15,000. It is widely accepted however that the annual number of notified addicts under-estimates the total population of users of notifiable drugs during that year. Local prevalence studies, using a variety of case-finding methods and conducted in different years have suggested that at times notifications may represent only 10−20 per cent of notifiable drug users, while in others 50 per cent of the users located were found to have been notified as addicts at some time. Given the extent of local variations both in the prevalence of drug misuse and in the numbers notified, changes over time in incidence rates in the same area, and the availability and effectiveness of treatment, our best guess is that there might have been between 75,000 and 150,000 misusers of notifiable drugs in the UK during 1986. In addition there may be as many again (excluding cannabis users) who are using a variety of non-notifiable drugs (such as amphetamine) on an experimental or occasional basis. Home Office statistics for 1986 show that there have been continuing annual increases in the quantity of amphetamine seized. In parallel with this, anecdotal evidence and local research studies suggest that amphetamine is now widely misused and may be the main drug of misuse in some areas. Moreover, use by injecting, on an occasional or regular basis is widely reported and appears to be on the increase.

1.14 Within this very broad picture of the scale of drug misuse, the pattern of misuse is complex. Many drug misusers will switch from one drug to another if their drug of first choice becomes too expensive or hard to obtain locally. Some misuse one drug at at time, others may be misusing several at any given time. Similar complexities apply to the method of administration. There are many shades of grey between a drug misuser who never injects and a drug misuser who always injects. Many people who misuse drugs primarily by inhalation or swallowing also inject drugs occasionally. One factor often mentioned here is price and availability: when a drug is scarce and expensive many misusers prefer to inject so as to maximise the effect of the limited amount they have been able to obtain. Most drug misusers in England begin their drug misuse by inhalation but many progress to injecting, probably passing through several stages. Halting this progression to injecting is of key importance in curbing the spread of HIV.

1.15 These variations in drug use and method of administration make it very hard to quantify the number of people who may be misusing drugs by injection. Anecdotal and research evidence up until mid-1987 suggests that, depending on the area studied, between 0 per cent and 90 per cent of opioid misuses may predominately use by injection. Over the country as a whole therefore, we have assumed that about half of all opioid misusers may at some time inject. On this basis, in 1986 there may have been between 37,000 (half of 75,000) and 75,000 (half of 150,000) injectors of notifiable drugs in the UK supplemented by a pool of injectors of other drugs (particularly amphetamines).

1.16 Reliable data on sharing of injecting equipment is also difficult to find but a number of recent studies with injecting drug misusers suggest that the vast majority have shared equipment at some time either regularly or occasionally. This was borne out by the anecdotal evidence presented by witnesses working with drug misusers. One recent study indicated a major drop in sharing amongst attenders at one London drug clinic and many witnesses from drug agencies reported reductions in sharing, though significant levels of sharing continued in many places. Another study, which preceded the Government's current publicity campaign, found little reduction in sharing amongst injecting misusers who are not in contact with services. Factors associated with sharing equipment require further study, but the non-availability of clean equipment (either generally, or just at the time and place of injection) and the view that sharing is the social norm in some drug injecting sub-cultures, are of importance.

1.17 In conclusion, the following points about the scale and pattern of drug misuse are important in devising a strategy to combat the spread of HIV:

a. during 1986 many misusers of certain controlled drugs were likely to do so by injection. Almost all of those who inject either regularly or occasionally will have shared equipment at some time and many continue to do so;

b. injecting drug use is not confined to the opioids; there is some research and anecdotal evidence that amphetamines and other drugs are also injected;

c. patterns of drug use, and method of administration, vary considerably over time between and within different areas;

d. injecting drug use is not confined to persistent regular injectors; a large number of misusers inject drugs occasionally while retaining inhalation or swallowing as their main method of use.

Preventing or halting an individual's progression from inhalation or swallowing to injection is an effective way of combating the spread of HIV.

2 Basic Principles

2.1 We discussed in Chapter 1 the potential threat posed by HIV and we have no hesitation in concluding that **the spread of HIV is a greater danger to individual and public health than drug misuse. Accordingly, services which aim to minimise HIV risk behaviour by all available means should take precedence in development plans.** We emphasise however, that the goals of minimising HIV risk behaviour and minimising drug misuse are compatible and that reducing injecting drug misuse is one of several strategies which will bear fruit in tackling the spread of the virus.

2.2 At both strategic and individual levels there are a number of approaches which will help to contain the spread of the virus through drug misuse:

- preventing or reducing injecting drug misuse;
- preventing or reducing sharing of injecting equipment;
- preventing or reducing unprotected sexual intercourse (involving injecting drug misusers – but also applicable of course to the population as a whole);
- advising infected women to avoid pregnancy and providing help where needed to reduce the number of births to those women.

Each of these approaches will have different degrees of success with different individuals. We must recognise each of them as a valid goal. In particular, we must recognise that, for the time being, many drug misusers will not be sufficiently motivated to consider abstinence and that many drug injectors will not be sufficiently motivated to change their route of administration. **We must therefore be prepared to work with those who continue to misuse drugs to help them reduce the risks involved in doing so, above all the risk of acquiring or spreading HIV.** Reaching this less well motivated group will necessitate a more proactive approach and a readiness to work initially towards goals which fall short of abstinence. This is essential if we are to make any significant impact in controlling the spread of HIV. There are however no 'master strokes' which will deliver the achievement of these goals. Patterns of drug misuse and sexual behaviour and the personal and situational factors which govern attitudes to risk taking, differ from one individual to another. A range of responses is needed to maximise the reduction in risk behaviour. The greatest benefit is more likely to accrue from the sum of multiple small gains deriving from an integrated and responsive total strategy than from any single approach.

2.3 In order to maximise the achievement of the goals in para 2.2 we need to get health education information to drug misusers, persuade them to change their behaviour, and provide them with the necessary help and support to achieve the required changes. Doing so will be much more difficult than it is proving with the homosexual community. Not only is the homosexual community stronger in its resources and networks of personal support, but the more enlightened social and legal attitudes to homosexuality which have developed over the last two or three decades have undoubtedly made it easier to reach and educate this community. The same cannot be said of attitudes to drug misuse, which remains the subject of great social stigma. As long as drug misusers see that drug misuse *per se* makes it more difficult to obtain primary health care, and attracts stiffer penalties from the courts, victimisation in prison and penalisation in the policies of public and commercial institutions, many will not come forward for help. The stigma attached to HIV and its association with drug misuse has exacerbated this problem. **We conclude that a change in professional and public attitudes to drug misuse is necessary as attitudes and policies which lead to drug misusers remaining hidden will impair the effectiveness of measures to combat the spread of HIV.** Ministers and other public figures can play a vital role by giving a strong lead in changing attitudes.

2.4 Turning to immediate practical measures we believe that the most effective way of changing the behaviour of many drug users involves first bringing them into personal contact with a helping agency. This view is supported by substantial evidence that agency contact is associated with more hygienic injecting practices amongst those who continue to inject. Chapter 3 describes the existing helping services and considers their ability to cope with present demand. Chapters 4, 5 and 6 go on to examine ways of bringing more users into contact with helping agencies and ways of changing their behaviour once contact has been established. Inevitably, whatever efforts are made, some drug misusers will remain out of contact with services. Chapter 5 includes discussion of measures that can be taken to influence them away from HIV risk behaviour.

2.5 This urgent report focuses very largely on reaching, and changing the behaviour of, those people who are already misusing drugs. It is right that it should do so since this group, particularly injectors (and their sexual partners), are at the most immediate risk of acquiring and spreading HIV. However, we emphasise that **prevention of drug misuse is now more important than ever before and in the longer run the success or failure of efforts to prevent young people from embarking on a career of drug misuse will have a major effect on our ability to contain the spread of HIV.**

3 Existing Services

3.1 This chapter provides a brief overview of the pattern of existing services for drug misusers and considers the ability of these services to respond to the demand they face.

The Advisory Council's Report on Treatment and Rehabilitation

3.2 The Advisory Council's report on Treatment and Rehabilitation was published in 1982. It highlighted the need for a comprehensive approach to drug misuse with the emphasis on a multi-disciplinary response, calling for active involvement of a wide range of both specialist and non-specialist agencies. It emphasised in particular, the need for the range of service provision to include:

a. *Hospital-Based Treatment Services*
Staffed by a multi-disciplinary team comprising at least a consultant psychiatrist, another doctor, a social worker, and a nurse. Able to undertake assessment and provide help from a full range of options which should include detoxification as an inpatient, outpatient or day patient, short or longer-term prescribing of controlled drugs or other medicines, referral where appropriate to a rehabilitation facility and counselling and treatment over a period of months or years. The need for active liaison with other specialist and non-specialist services was stressed.

b. *Other Specialist Agencies*
Three kinds of services were identified as important here. First, advice and counselling services which should aim to assist individuals to contain their drug misuse and, where necessary, to accept further help. Second, day care which was seen as a means of providing a more structured and therapeutic environment for drug misusers. Third, residental facilities for drug misusers including supported accommodation for those continuing to take drugs and drug-free accommodation for those needing a therapeutic residential unit to adjust to abstinence.

21

c. *Non-Specialist Services*

Primary medical services, social services departments, the probation service, housing departments and housing associations, employment services and non-specialist, non-statutory agencies were all identified as having a valuable role to play. The opportunities these services provide to intervene with drug problems at an early stage were highlighted.

3.3 The report recommended that this range of services should be supported by multi-disciplinary Drug Problem Teams established initially at Regional level, and in the longer term at District level. The establishment of Drug Advisory Committees at both Regional and District levels was also recommended, to monitor the prevalence of drug misuse and the effectiveness of services and to foster improvements.

Developments Since 1982

3.4 In response to the report, the Government funded a major expansion in services for drug misusers. In England, £17.5 million was committed to a Central Funding Initiative which provided 'pump-priming' funds for 188 local projects. Forty-two per cent of the projects funded were in the voluntary sector and almost half the funding went to community-based services. This central funding was provided for a maximum of 3 years with the intention that statutory authorities should pick up the funding at the end of the period, providing the service remained relevant to local needs. First indications are that funding has been picked up locally in the vast majority of cases where central funding has expired, though the overall numbers of such cases are currently small. Since 1985–86 the DHSS has provided health authorities in England with £5 million a year to continue the development of local services and in 1987–88 a further £1 million was provided to help drug misuse services to play a growing role in tackling AIDS and HIV.

3.5 Central funding was also provided in Scotland and Wales. In Wales since 1985–86 £1.64m has been allocated to District Health Authorities and voluntary bodies for the development of services for drug misusers. Funding is on a recurrent basis for the duration of projects, subject to a review after 3 years that the services continue to be needed and are effective. Recently, the Welsh Office received bids from district health authorities for funds to support AIDS prevention activities, and funds (£33,500 pa) have been made available specifically for the counselling of drug misusers. In Scotland, funds have been set aside in the health programme since 1984–85 specifically for the support of drug misuse services. From 1987–88, over £1 million per annum is being made available for this purpose and Health Boards have assumed responsibility for the local projects previously funded by the Scottish Home and Health Department.

3.6 More details can be found in papers submitted to us by the Health Departments which are reproduced at Annex E.

The Present State of Services

3.7 Our enquiries, together with the evidence submitted to us, show that there has undoubtedly been a major expansion and development of services since the report on Treatment and Rehabilitation was published. We particularly welcome the very significant increase in community-based facilities. We also welcome the increased specialist psychiatric input which has occurred in many areas through, for example, more use of community psychiatric nurses as well as new consultant posts. The combination of community services and medical input in the Community Drug Teams which some districts have established, particularly in the North West, is an important development. There are, however, significant variations in the services available in different districts and regions. In some areas, the service provision is minimal and expansion is urgently needed.

3.8 Just as important as the scale of service provision is the range of services and help available. Here again, the picture varies considerably across the UK. In some areas positive and enthusiastic attitudes have led to a full range of co-ordinated services being provided. In others, entrenched attitudes have contributed to incomplete and ill-co-ordinated provision of services. Three points in particular cause us grave concern:

a. the refusal of many psychiatrists in Scotland to accept more than a very limited role in the treatment of drug misuse;

b. the failure of specialist services in some areas to provide help from the full range of options, including prescribing options, described in the Treatment and Rehabilitation report (and reproduced at para 3.2(a) above); and

c. the reluctance of many general practitioners, and other generic professionals, to accept the identification and treatment of drug misusers as part of their role.

We believe that these shortcomings must be rectified if services are to be fully effective in tackling the spread of HIV. We return to each of them later in this report.

3.9 We have not been able to conduct a comprehensive survey of the demand on services but the evidence we have received suggests that most services are already working at, or beyond, their capacity. Several witnesses have explained that their services no longer actively seek new clients as they are already overburdened and there are some long waiting times for hospital-based specialist treatment.

3.10 In conclusion, we welcome the major expansion of services for drug misusers resulting from Government action and funding following the publication of the Treatment and Rehabilitation report. Those areas which have developed services in accordance with the Treatment and Rehabilitation report and subsequent Government guidance will be best placed to implement the further developments now needed to combat the spread of HIV. In other areas, where services are less well developed, urgent action is required to rectify shortcomings and provide a base for the new developments needed to tackle HIV. **In all areas, substantial further expansion will be necessary if services are to reach more drug misusers and play an effective role in curbing the spread of HIV.**

4 Maximising Contact with Drug Misusers

4.1 We discuss in this chapter ways in which more drug misusers can be brought into contact with helping services. The next chapter looks at ways of bringing about behaviour change once contact has been established. The distinction is a slightly artificial one which is made here for ease of presentation: we do not advocate increasing contact for its own sake but in order to provide the opportunity to inform and influence behaviour. The issue of prescribing, which we believe is relevant both to maximising contact and changing behaviour, is discussed in Chapter 6.

Extent of Contact with Services

4.2 Chapter 1 notes the difficulty in establishing how many people are misusing drugs at any given time. In addition, there is no centrally held information about the total number of drug users in contact with helping services; the only such data relates to misusers seen, and notified, by doctors. Local studies do however provide some insights and the evidence we have received suggests that the proportion of opiate misusers in touch with helping services at any given time is in the 5 per cent to 20 per cent range. Misusers of stimulants (mainly amphetamines) are generally much less likely to be in contact with services than opiate misusers. Clearly, the picture will differ between localities according to the nature of local drug services and the local drug problem but undoubtedly, the large majority of opiate and stimulant misusers are not in contact with helping services. Of this large majority, some will have been in touch in the past but have broken contact either temporarily or permanently, others will never have sought help. Whilst some of those who have not sought help will be relatively new to drug misuse, evidence shows that others will have been misusing drugs regularly for many years.

4.3 This low level of contact with services must be seen against a background of services having been developed primarily to help 'problem drug takers'[1]. Many drug misusers may not think of themselves as having a drug problem, nor may they experience drug-related problems (e.g. with health, money, the law). **The advent of HIV requires an expansion of our definition of problem drug use to include any form of drug misuse which involves, or may lead to, the sharing of injecting equipment. This in turn means that services must now make contact with as many of the hidden population of drug misusers as possible.** (See Annex D).

Factors Affecting Contact with Services

4.4 There are a range of factors which influence the extent to which drug misusers make and maintain contact with helping services. For many of those who currently seek help, motivating factors in doing so often include concern about dependence, depression, legal, health, employment, accommodation and financial problems, and worries over relationships. Whether motivation results in contact actually being made depends on factors such as the type of service available locally, the individual's knowledge of local services, the accessibility of services, and whether the individual perceives the service as accepting of, and relevant to, their needs.

4.5 A strategy to maximise the number of drug misusers who make contact with services must therefore include:

- additional motivation to seek help
- the provision of services which are relevant to the needs and problems of potential clients
- effective dissemination of information about the existence and nature of the services
- easy accessibility of services
- non-threatening services.

4.6 Taking each of these factors in turn:

a. *Additional Motivation*
Evidence from many parts of the country indicates that AIDS, and the publicity surrounding it, is influencing an increasing number of drug misusers to seek help. This trend needs to be reinforced by continued pub-

---

[1] Defined in the 1982 Treatment and Rehabilitation Report as: 'Any person who experiences social, psychological, physical or legal problems related to intoxication and/or regular excessive consumption and/or dependence as a consequence of his own use of drugs or other chemical substances (excluding alcohol and tobacco).

licity both nationally and locally. However, there is also a need to develop positive motivation to seek help. Evidence suggests that contact with helping agencies and commitment to behaviour change is most effectively achieved when an individual can identify real benefits through such contact. Local publicity is particularly important here as it can not only provide motivation but also give details of the help available locally. Better information (see (c) below) and the development of accessible services can contribute to increasing motivation and providing additional grounds for seeking help. Finally, drug misusers who have made contact with a helping service can be an important source of information to other drug misusers about that service. Influencing those drug misusers to promote a positive image of the benefits of the service can encourage other drug misusers to seek help.

b. *Relevant Services*
Services must be relevant to those whose principal motivation is avoiding HIV and AIDS as well as those who are motivated to seek help in reducing their drug misuse. Advice and help with risk-reduction for those who continue to misuse drugs is therefore essential. Availability of advice and practical help with other problems which drug misusers often face will offer an additional incentive for drug misusers to contact helping services. Common problems include areas such as housing, welfare benefits and finance generally, primary health care, employment/training, the law and child care.

c. *Dissemination of Information*
Even amongst drug misusers who seek help many do not know about the full range of helping agencies in the area nor do they have an accurate image of the service available. Knowledge and perceptions amongst those who have no contact with an agency is still more limited and clouded. More detailed and imaginative local publicity is needed to inform drug misusers of the existence of agencies and the type of help available, and to dispel their fears about seeking help. Local publicity must emphasise that help in avoiding HIV is available to those who do not yet feel motivated to reduce their drug misuse.

d. *Accessibility*
Easy accessibility is important even for drug misusers who are highly motivated to seek help. Now that services must make contact with many who are not so highly motivated it is all the more important. Easy access by public transport is essential. Flexible opening hours may also help, particularly in reaching drug misusers who are in work. Waiting times are

also highly significant: if drug misusers are kept waiting a long time for an appointment, or kept waiting when they arrive at the agency, their motivation is likely to fade and they may break contact.

e. *Non-threatening Services*
In general, services which are run by sympathetic, non-judgemental staff in informal community-based settings may be seen as less threatening than those sited in hospital premises which may convey an authoritarian image. In addition to this general point there are two specific fears amongst some drug misusers: first, fear of the notification process and second, fear that their drug misuse may lead to their children being taken into care. There is conflicting evidence about the deterrent effect of the notification procedure but it does appear to act as a deterrent to some of those who might otherwise seek help. Similarly, worries over child care do seem to deter some drug misusing parents from seeking help particularly from any source associated with authority (see also para 4.20). These specific fears reinforce the need for additional services separate from formal or hospital-sited services.

Developing the Pattern of Service Provision

4.7 In the light of the considerations above, we do not see hospital-sited services as offering the most appropriate focus for attracting significant numbers of new clients from the hidden population of drug misusers. Community-based services have a greater chance of reaching many elements of this population by the provision of more varied and acceptable sources of help and advice. General practitioners can also play a key role as readily accessible points of contact who are well placed to help drug misusers move towards safer practices. This does not mean that the role of the hospital-sited specialist treatment unit is in any way diminished; on the contrary, these units can provide vital support for primary services and have important contributions to make in combating the spread of HIV. The role of each of these types of service along with that of generic services and outreach work is discussed below.

Community-Based Services

4.8 In the light of the conclusions reached earlier in this chapter we consider that community-based drug services should be substantially developed and expanded. In addition to their present role of providing services to 'problem' drug misusers it is now essential that they should reach drug misusers who do not perceive themselves as having a drug problem. In order to do so they will need to adopt a more positive approach to attracting and contacting drug misusers than has hitherto been necessary. They will also need to provide services which are relevant to people who continue to misuse drugs and particularly to help them avoid acquiring or transmitting HIV. This represents a major extension to the role of existing community-based drug services. This expanded role is illustrated in more detail in the pattern of community-based developments outlined in Annex C, and developed in Chapter 5, which examines the issues of advice on risk-reduction, supply of injecting equipment, and antibody testing, and Chapter 6 which looks at prescribing. **We recommend that a pattern of community-based services, along the lines of that outlined at Annex C, should be available in each health district.**

4.9 Some of the community-based drug services which have developed over the last few years provide many of the ingredients we have identified as important and could be developed as outlined in Annex C. Other such services could not easily adapt to this model but may nevertheless continue to do valuable work. Annex C does not provide a standard model to be followed by all community-based drug agencies but every drug misuser should have access to the type of service described. District Drug Advisory Committees will be best placed to determine with service providers which services can be adapted and/or whether entirely new services need to be established. Either way, a major expansion of provision will be needed so that many more drug misusers can be reached. Where an existing service is adapted, publicising the new features of the service will be especially important. We emphasise that these services constitute one element of the service provision needed in each District: they do not represent a complete response in themselves. Their place in the overall pattern of services needed to combat the spread of HIV through drug misuse is illustrated at Annex D.

General Practitioners

4.10 The network of general practitioners offers an unrivalled system of heath care provision with great opportunities for intervention with drug misusing patients. GPs and the primary health care team, including health visitors, are particularly well placed to intervene early in cases of substance misuse and to work with families in helping misusers to move away from dangerous behaviour and towards abstinence. It has been estimated recently that between 30 and 44 thousand new opioid misusers in England and Wales consult general practitioners each year. These opportunities for intervention have not yet been adequately seized in most areas. Evidence suggests that some GPs are unwilling to provide health care for drug misusers and that many others do not provide help with drug problems. GP involvement is often considerably greater in areas where support is available through community drug teams or other specialist drug services and this is clearly a desirable arrangement. **We conclude that the advent of HIV makes it essential that all GPs should provide care and advice for drug misusing patients to help move them away from behaviour which may result in them acquiring and spreading the virus. Health authorities should ensure that appropriate support is available and that GPs are made aware of it.**

4.11 General practitioners already possess the skills needed to help drug misusers but some may need to improve their confidence and knowledge of the field through further training. Training which facilitates early identification of, and intervention in, drug misuse is particularly important. The Council's forthcoming report on training will make recommendations about GPs' training needs and how they can be met. We note that some GPs have obtained valuable training and experience in the field through clinical attachments to local specialist drug services (as recommended in the Council's report on Treatment and Rehabilitation). **We consider that such attachments should be actively encouraged and recommend that short-term (e.g. 6–12 months) sessional contracts should be available to help build a pool of GPs with this experience. Wherever possible, their medical contribution should be provided with the support and advice of a consultant with special expertise in drug dependence.**

4.12 In the longer term, the best opportunity to promote greater involvement of all doctors is through training. We recommend that all doctors should receive some training at undergraduate level and postgraduate level on the problem and management of drug misuse. Further training for GPs should also be provided at postgraduate level both during the three-year vocational training period and for established practitioners on a regular basis.

4.13 The recent White Paper 'Promoting Better Health' emphasises the need for GPs and primary health care teams to play an increasing role in health promotion and preventive medicine. Clearly GPs can play a vital role in preventing the spread of HIV infection by increasing their contacts and involvement with drug misusers. The White Paper proposes that a new postgraduate educational allowance should be available to GPs who maintain a regular programme of education and training throughout their career. Discussions of the range and provision of approved training courses should recognize the importance of enhancing the expertise and involvement of more GPs in working with drug misusers.

4.14 Once contact between a drug misuser and a GP has been established, the principles described in Chapter 5 (Changing Behaviour) and Chapter 6 (Prescribing) will play an important part within the context of the care that a GP may provide.

Hospital-based specialist services

4.15 Hospital-based specialist services play two important roles. First, they provide essential back-up for 'front-line' drug agencies and GPs. Second, they can play an important role in attracting some drug misusers directly and in helping them move away from HIV risk behaviour.

4.16 The need for, and role of, hospital-based treatment services was discussed in the Council's report on Treatment and Rehabilitation (see particularly para 6.25 of that report). The back-up these services provide, through giving advice and accepting referrals, is critical to the smooth running of front-line agencies. If this more specialist support is not available the capacity of front-line agencies and GPs can be quickly sapped by a small number of the most difficult cases. We have heard evidence of this happening in Scotland, where psychiatrists play only a very limited role in the treatment of drug misuse; as a result front-line agencies are working under immense strain. It is also clear that some hospital-based specialist services have such long waiting times (6 weeks or more) that they do not provide realistic back-up for other services. **We emphasise that if 'front-line' services are to be successful in making contact with more drug misusers the support available from hospital-based specialist services will need to be expanded and strengthened. Such support must be available in every District backed up by more specialist Regional support as outlined in the Treatment and Rehabilitation Report.** In some areas, particularly Scotland which we discuss in Chapter 10, major improvements are needed urgently.

4.17 Although hospital-sited services are not best placed to attract new clients in large numbers they should nonetheless take steps to improve their accessibility and acceptability. There are two aspects to this:

– making other professionals more aware of their service and how best to make use of it; and

– making the service more accessible and acceptable to clients so that drug misusers, whether referred by other professionals or not, are more likely to make and maintain contact.

Many of the suggestions in the guidelines for community-based services (Annex C) will apply to some degree to hospital-based services. **We recommend in particular:**

a. *Better dissemination of information*
This needs to cover both the existence of the service and clear details of the type of help available. It should be aimed both at 'front-line' drug workers (including GPs), at other professionals including hospital staff, particularly those working in Accident and Emergency Departments, and at drug misusers themselves. Initiatives such as open days, annual reports, talks to groups of GPs and other generic workers should be considered. Better publicity about specialist units and their role should, if properly handled, encourage GPs and other generic professionals to become more involved in the field.

b. *Flexible opening hours*
Evening opening may be important for drug misusers who are in work. There is evidence of working drug misusers being expected to attend clinics daily in working hours to collect prescriptions or participate in psycho-therapy. If regular attendance is essential then ways should be found of making it compatible with the client's employment. Some drug clinics already operate flexible hours for such clients and we commend this approach. This flexibility should be well publicised so that potential clients are not put off accepting referral.

c. *Minimising waiting times*
This refers both to waiting times for appointments and the time between first appointment and commencement of treatment. The former is largely a matter of adequate resources but a review of working practices may nevertheless reveal some scope for reducing any initial waiting period. It is of course important to ensure that the specialist services do not become silted up with patients who could be adequately managed by GPs and/or community-based services. Regular reviews of each patient and good working relationships with other service providers are important. The question of time-lag before treatment is discussed in relation to prescribing at 6.10.

Generic services

4.18 Some services which are not drug-orientated nevertheless come into contact with large numbers of drug misusers. Examples include social services, youth services, the probation service and some non-statutory agencies (e.g. those which focus on the problems of the young or homeless). These services can play an important role in identifying drug misusers amongst their clients, and providing advice, counselling and referral to specialist agencies. The report on Treatment and Rehabilitation discussed this role. **In the light of HIV early identification and intervention by these agencies is of heightened importance.** Equally, these agencies now need to be equipped to give advice on HIV and safer practice (see Chapter 5).

4.19 The Probation Service in particular is likely to have a high level of contact with drug misusers many of whom will have no other contact with a helping agency. The proposals at 8.19 for diversion from prison will rely considerably on the involvement of probation officers and their ability to direct drug misusers towards appropriate helping services. However, many drug misusers will not receive a supervision order and there will be an important role for probation officers as health educators about means of reducing the risk of HIV infection and in increasing motivation to seek help amongst those drug misusers who may have only brief contact with the probation service.

4.20 Social Services Departments should be aware that drug misusing parents may be particularly wary of disclosing their drug use to social workers for fear that their children will be taken into care. A Local Authority has a duty to act in the best interests of a child's welfare but drug use by parents does not automatically indicate child neglect or abuse and it is important that fear that their children will be taken into care should not deter parents from coming forward for assistance. Social Services workers can play an important part in increasing parenting capabilities and supporting such parents with advice, guidance and practical services and there should be improved liaison between generic and specialised services. Drug misuse agencies may be unaware of or unfamiliar with resources and practices within generic agencies and this may reinforce a client's fears at a time when multi-agency support is needed. **If drug misusing parents are not to be deterred from seeking help, Social Services Departments should work hard to ensure that drug misuse *per se* is never, and is never seen as, a reason for separating parent and child.**

4.21 Another service which is likely to come into contact with increasing numbers of drug misusers as a result of HIV is the Genito Urinary Medicine

(GUM) clinic. Many drug misusers who attend GUM clinics for antibody testing have been referred by drug services and are therefore already receiving some help with their drug problem. However, other drug misusers may present without referral. It is extremely important that staff at GUM clinics should be fully equipped to advise drug misusers about safe practices and to encourage them to seek help with their drug problem. This will apply, whether the result is positive or not. We recommend that staff in GUM clinics should develop streamlined arrangements for referring clients to drug services. In some clinics where large numbers of drug misusers are seen the provision of an on-site drugs worker should be considered. GUM clinics should further advertise the availability of HIV counselling and testing and these services should be made more easily accessible. Although we believe the antibody test should be used with caution (see Chapter 5) it is clearly desirable that as many drug misusers as possible come forward for HIV counselling and that the opportunities presented when they do so are seized. Many GUM clinics are already over-stretched with the advent of HIV and additional space, resources and staffing will be required to enable them to play their proper role.

4.22 Other professionals may also have contact with drug misusers, albeit of a more casual nature. Examples include pharmacists, police officers and staff of Accident and Emergency Departments. We note that the Pharmaceutical Society of Great Britain has recently distributed a handbook on drug misuse to its members and we commend this initiative. Some information on identifying and helping drug misusers should be part of the basic training of all professionals who are likely to have contact with them.

Outreach work

4.23 Finally in this chapter, we consider the role of outreach work as a means of making contact with drug misusers. This form of work has a long tradition in making contact with young people unwilling to use established 'centre-based' services, most notably in the youth service. The goal of outreach work has often been to involve young people in existing services, but more recently it has been developed to provide a direct service to those unwilling to utilise existing resources.

4.24 Outreach workers have been employed in a number of countries to work with drug misusers, especially in a number of European countries. These services have now been extended to contact drug misusers and provide them with information about HIV and safer practices, notably in the USA. In some places, the approach has focused largely on the provision of bleach and advice on cleaning equipment, in others, advice on safer practices has been the main focus. Contact has been developed largely on the street and in locations where drug misusers are known to meet. In many cases, former injecting drug misusers have been recruited as outreach workers because of their knowledge of the drug scene. In all cases, outreach work has proved a valuable tool in making contact with those not willing to approach services. It has, however, been dependent on the skills and qualities of the workers, on establishment of trust between them and the drug misusers and on the ability to relate to clients on their own terms and in settings of their choosing.

4.25 There are only a few examples of outreach work with drug misusers being undertaken in the UK. One of these is in Strathclyde where with SHHD funding the Social Work Department established six detached drug-worker posts. The emphasis here has been on making and maintaining contacts with drug misusers and their families, providing advice and counselling, including risk-reduction, and helping drug misusers to make use of other services. In some cases it proved easy to establish contacts, but workers in other areas experienced difficulties. An important lesson to emerge was the desirability of operating in teams for mutual support and safety, with an established base and well-defined routes of referral to other helping agencies.

4.26 Strathclyde Regional Council has also undertaken outreach work with prostitutes, a particularly important group as a significant proportion in that area are also drug misusers. Here the emphasis was primarily on the need to avoid unprotected sex. It was found that some prostitutes were willing to help in this work and could be most effective in distributing condoms and advice about safer sexual practices. Nevertheless, drug misusing prostitutes represented a particular problem since they seemed to be more willing to have unprotected sex, especially if offered extra money. Those who engage in casual prostitution when they need money for drugs are likely to be the most difficult to reach through any network of prostitutes.

4.27 The examples of outreach work in mainland Europe, the USA and some parts of the UK, suggest that there is potential in using current and former drug misusers and prostitutes as voluntary or informal 'outreach workers' in conjunction with staff employed specifically as outreach workers. The experience of non-statutory street agencies and rehabilitation houses has already shown the benefit of employing former drug users within their services.

4.28 We conclude that the type of community-based services we advocate earlier in this chapter will, if implemented with enthusiasm and imagination, reach a larger proportion of drug misusers than is presently in contact with services. Outreach workers can play an additional role in contacting drug misusers who may not otherwise seek help, for instance, young drug misusers, drug misusing prostitutes, occasional drug misusers and amphetamine misusers. Such work can only be fully effective if backed up by the full range of services outlined in this report. We note the value of undertaking outreach work as part of a team and suggest that community-based drug services would form a natural base for these teams. Health and local authorities should consider collaborating with neighbouring authorities in building such teams, drawing upon the experience of detached youth work. Former drug misusers or prostitutes may be particularly effective as outreach workers because of their knowledge and experience and the trust which they can more readily establish with current misusers. Health and local authorities should ensure that there are no bars to such candidates being appointed as full-time, sessional or volunteer staff at the appropriate grading for similar posts within the authority.

4.29 Beyond these basic points, we consider that the exact model used for outreach work will differ according to local circumstances. The possibility of using regular clients of drug services to disseminate information about HIV and safe practices should not be overlooked as a means of reaching, at a basic level, drug misusers who remain unwilling to make contact with any helping service. **We recommend that drug services experiment with a variety of approaches, and monitor carefully their effectiveness in reaching drug misusers not in touch with services, and in conveying help and advice.**

5 Changing Behaviour

5.1 We have discussed the action we consider necessary to bring more drug misusers into contact with services. In this chapter we examine steps which can be taken to change their behaviour once contact has been established. We also discuss briefly how the behaviour of those who remain out of contact can be influenced.

A Hierarchy of goals

5.2 Chapter 2 referred to the need for services to work with those who continue to misuse drugs to help them reduce the risk of spreading or acquiring HIV. Here we suggest that services need to adopt a hierarchy of goals in dealing with drug misusers and to accept that, at any given time, different goals may be appropriate for different individuals. Thus, with regard to drug misuse, the following goals will all reduce the risk to the individual and to others:

a. becoming drug free
b. switching from injecting to oral use
c. avoiding sharing equipment.

Drug misusers cannot be allocated to simple categories of 'wanting to give up drugs' or 'not wanting to give up drugs', or of 'wanting to change' or 'not wanting to change'. Drug misusers will be found to exist somewhere on a continuum between these extremes and to show an ambivalent attitude. Services should therefore strongly encourage drug misusers towards a goal of abstinence, but for drug misusers who are not immediately motivated to give up, goals (b) and (c) will be more realistic for the time being. Thus drug services must be prepared to help one client to give up drugs entirely whilst advising the next client on how to minimise the risks of continued drug use. We see these goals as complementary, not contradictory, and we draw an analogy with advice on cigarette smoking. In this allied field it is widely accepted that advice on reducing the risk of continued smoking by switching to low-tar and filter cigarettes must exist alongside the advice on the greater benefit of cessation of smoking entirely.

5.3 The different goals for drug misusers must not be seen as in competition. Care must be taken when advising on avenues to abstinence to ensure that advice is given on ways of reducing the risk in the event of on-going use or a return to use. Likewise, advice on risk-reduction with regard to on-going use must not encourage continued use and should where possible increase awareness of the greater benefit from abstinence as and when that may be achieved.

5.4 Alongside these goals related to drug misuse lies the important goal of preventing spread of HIV through sexual activity. Here, the same considerations apply as with the population generally but there are three additional special factors:

a. injecting drug misusers who have shared equipment may be at greater risk of already being infected;

b. some drug misusers finance their use of drugs through prostitution;

c. drug misusers may be less likely to heed general publicity about sexual transmission.

Advice and Counselling on Risk-Reduction

5.5 We were encouraged to learn from the evidence we received that many services in contact with drug misusers are giving advice on HIV risk-reduction and in the main they reported few difficulties in doing so. The advice given covered safer injecting (in terms of HIV), safer sex, availability of injecting equipment and, in some cases, cleaning of equipment. The concept of advice on abstinence and risk-reduction existing side by side does not seem to be creating practical problems. The evidence suggests that contact with a helping agency, and advice on safer practices, can be effective in reducing the sharing of equipment, particularly when there is easy access to clean injecting equipment. There is much less evidence of changes in sexual behaviour (see below).

5.6 Drug misusers who are not thought to be injecting must not be overlooked when advice is given on AIDS and the need to avoid shared injecting. Evidence from several sources suggests that drug misusers who state that they are inhaling or swallowing may also be injecting occasionally. Even if they have not yet injected they may well mix with others who do inject and may encourage them to try. Any injecting which does occur amongst this group is very likely to involve someone else's equipment. It is essential that these individuals should be warned about the dangers of shared injecting and how to avoid them. Similar considerations apply to those who are receiving prescribed oral preparations.

5.7 Advice on safer sex seems to be more problematical for some staff to give and for many drug misusers to follow. Many staff who work with drug misusers have little previous experience in discussing sexual matters and find it difficult to do so particularly with clients who have come to discuss their drug problem rather than their sex life. Moreover, many drug misusers are reluctant to talk about sexual matters. Some agencies have found it easier to cover sex as part of a general discussion on health care; others try to build a rapport with the client first. A significant number of callers at helping agencies call only once or twice however, and it is therefore essential that the opportunity to provide advice on safer sex (and safer practices generally) is seized as early as possible. Service managers should ensure that all staff working with drug misusers (including those in the voluntary sector) have access to training on sexual counselling. This may be provided either through formal courses or informally using staff experienced in this field (e.g. GUM or Family Planning staff).

5.8 All staff who come into contact with drug misusers can play a part in providing information on AIDS and the need for safer practices. In some cases this may simply involve the provision of a leaflet (such as the SCODA leaflet – 'AIDS – How Drug Users can avoid it') by, for example, a police officer or pharmacist. Where possible, details of the local drug service should also be provided. In other cases, there may be an opportunity for a generic or drug-specialist worker to discuss the subject during a one-off contact. In cases of prolonged contact it should be possible to raise the subject on a number of occasions and discuss what progress the individual concerned is making.

5.9 **In conclusion, we recommend that all services in contact with drug misusers should inform them of the risks of HIV and how they can avoid and reduce these risks both sexual and of injecting.**

Provisions of Condoms and Injecting Equipment

5.10 Many drug services are providing drug misusers with free condoms obtained either from the Family Planning Clinic or direct from the health authority. We commend this move as reinforcing advice on safer sex and providing the means with which to practise it. **We recommend that all services for drug misusers, including general practitioners, should have the facility to provide free condoms.**

5.11 The question of provision of injecting equipment is more complex. Earlier this year, the Government set up fifteen pilot syringe exchange schemes in different parts of the UK. As well as providing new injecting equipment on an exchange basis these schemes give information on HIV and safer practices and offer counselling for drug problems. A larger number of similar schemes have been set up independently by health authorities and drug agencies. In addition, since February 1986 community pharmacists have been advised by their professional body that they may, at their discretion, sell needles and syringes to drug misusers: anecdotal evidence suggests that whilst significant numbers of pharmacists are willing to sell equipment, availability of equipment through this outlet is patchy.

5.12 Early findings from the monitoring of the pilot syringe exchange projects indicate that some exchange schemes can be successful in attracting drug misusers who are not otherwise in touch with helping services. Other schemes however have not attracted significant numbers of clients (Chapter 4 discusses the sort of features which seem to make services generally more attractive). No systematic data are yet available on behaviour change of those attending the schemes, though witnesses involved in exchange schemes have reported a major reduction in sharing.

5.13 Exchange schemes have been established in other parts of the world, most notably in Amsterdam where they have been running for some years. Research on the effects of the Amsterdam schemes is inconclusive: whilst there is a reported reduction in sharing overall since they have been running there is no apparent difference in sharing rates between those using the schemes and others. However, the schemes' users make up a large proportion of the city's injectors as a whole and the schemes may be indirectly responsible for changes in sharing amongst non-clients.

5.14 In some countries needles and syringes can be readily purchased at low cost in shops or supermarkets. Two such countries (Italy and Spain) have very high prevalence of HIV and AIDS amongst drug misusers. However, the virus had already spread widely in these countries before drug misusers were made aware of the risks of sharing. We do not therefore regard these countries' experiences as evidence that ready availability of injecting equipment need be associated with the spread of HIV where health education is provided. It should be noted that HIV spread extremely rapidly in Edinburgh when needles and syringes were in short supply.

5.15 The basic argument in favour of improving needle and syringe availability is that some drug misusers will inject come what may; making clean equipment readily accessible to them will reduce the likelihood of them sharing. This appears to be borne out by evidence from areas where the availability of equipment is limited – the result seems to be more sharing rather than less injecting. The basic counter-argument is that readier access to sterile equipment will encourage more drug misusers to start injecting or inject on a more regular basis thus creating a larger pool of injectors. The argument continues that since sharing will never be completely eliminated, as some injectors will share regardless of the hazards and that others will do so occasionally in an emergency, this will increase the size of the population at risk of acquiring and spreading HIV. This argument gains some support from a recent survey of non-injecting drug misusers 21 per cent of whom said they would start injecting if sterile equipment were easily available.

5.16 It is difficult to weigh the benefits of the possible reduction in sharing against the drawback of a possible increase in the size of the population at risk. The pilot syringe exchange projects will help provide more systematic evidence of the reported reduction in sharing. But any increase in injecting is likely to remain hidden. We see no prospect of these pilot schemes, or any other experiments, providing conclusive evidence in the forseeable future about their overall effectiveness in combating the spread of HIV. Yet the need for preventive action is urgent. In the light of the limited research and anecdotal evidence, and direct experience of working with drug misusers, our judgement is that the benefits of reduced sharing which will occur if needles and syringes are made readily available alongside health education will outweigh the risks involved in any increase in the injecting population which may result. We consider that the very existence of syringe exchange schemes also plays a valuable role in broadcasting to all drug misusers that sharing equipment is dangerous. **We recommend that further exchange schemes be set up drawing on the experience of the more successful pilot projects. Monitoring of these schemes should continue so that their success in reaching drug misusers and changing their behaviour can be assessed. For some drug misusers behaviour change may take several months to occur and these schemes should not be judged wholly by short-term results. Ultimately they must be judged on lasting evidence of behaviour change.**

5.17 Other things being equal, exchange of equipment is preferable to over-the-counter sales since it helps to ensure that new equipment is issued only to existing injectors and that used equipment is properly disposed of. It also provides greater opportunities for education about HIV and safer practices and counselling for drug problems. However, many injecting drug misusers will not be reached by exchange schemes either because they cannot be sufficiently local or because they are perceived as in some way threatening. The present scheme in Glasgow is an extreme example since it is hospital-based, guarded by a picket of local residents, and can issue only three syringes at a time. In the light of these drawbacks it may not be surprising that just one local pharmacist sells many times more syringes than the scheme manages to give away free. However, at the other extreme, the schemes which have been most successful in attracting clients would certainly not claim to have reached anything like the majority of local injectors. The sale of equipment through community pharmacies will therefore remain an important outlet for those injectors who are not within easy reach of an exchange scheme or will only accept the anonymity of a simple commercial transaction. **We recommend that community pharmacists should be encouraged to sell equipment at reasonable cost to injecting drug misusers and that, wherever possible, pharmacists should advise customers about any local exchange facility, encourage the use of condoms, and provide health education and information on local facilities for drug misusers by provision of leaflets and, where possible, by verbal advice. Health authorities should provide pharmacists, on request and free of charge, with disposal facilities for used equipment and pharmacists should encourage customers to return used equipment.**

5.18 **We recommend that all syringes should bear an indelible warning about the danger of sharing injecting equipment. The Government should discuss with syringe manufacturers how this can be achieved as soon as possible.**

5.19 Finally, we recognise that the pattern of injecting and existing needle and syringe availability is different in different areas. The action needed locally will depend on these local circumstances. In some areas, where injecting is prevalent and equipment is in short supply, immediate action will be needed to increase the supply. In other areas, where many pharmacists sell equipment and there may already be an exchange scheme, efforts might need to focus on advertising the availability of equipment. We caution against preconceptions about local circumstances and refer to the example of Liverpool where the scale of the local injecting problem came to light only after an exchange scheme was established. It will be important to secure the co-operation of local police forces in drawing up local arrangements for supply of equipment. **We recommend that District Drug**

Advisory Committees and Local Pharmaceutical Committees should immediately agree a plan for ensuring and advertising the availability of injecting equipment in the light of local circumstances. Local police should be consulted on and should co-operate with the agreed plan, to ensure that police activity does not discourage drug misusers from obtaining sterile equipment and/or returning equipment.

HIV Antibody Testing

5.20 There are many complexities surrounding HIV antibody testing. In this report we confine ourselves to considering what role it can play in combating the spread of HIV through injecting drug misuse. Chapter 4 discussed the possible value of antibody testing facilities in making contact with drug misusers. Here we consider the possible value of the test in bringing about changes towards safer behaviour.

5.21 The obvious problem with the antibody test as a tool in changing behaviour is that the same advice about safer behaviour applies to those found antibody positive, those found antibody negative and those who are untested. The evidence we have received indicated that the reactions of drug misusers to the results of tests vary tremendously. Amongst those found antibody negative responses range from carrying on as before to being motivated towards abstinence or a safer method of drug use. Reactions to a positive result often include fear, anxiety, depression, shock, anger, guilt and bewilderment. For some, the shock may act as a springboard to rehabilitation; for others concern about infecting other people or about increasing the risk of developing AIDS may lead to the adoption of some risk-reduction. But there is also evidence of many cases where a positive result has led to no behaviour change or to a marked deterioration. In some such cases anxiety/depression has led to increased drug misuse with chaotic, self-destructive behaviour. There have been cases of suicide and deliberate overdosing. Some antibody positive drug misusers have displayed indifference to infecting others.

5.22 This range of possible reactions highlights the need for caution before undertaking an antibody test and for proper pre- and post-test counselling. The counselling should explore whether the client really wants to know the result or is simply hoping to be found antibody negative, and how she/he would react to either result. It should also explain the implications of the result including:

- the limitations of the test
- the distinction between AIDS and HIV positivity
- current views on likelihood of progression
- current treatment approaches including their availability and limitations
- the significance of co-factors in developing AIDS, particularly the need to avoid injecting drugs (especially with shared equipment) and exposure to other infections (especially sexually transmitted ones)
- the possible psychological effect of a positive result and the effect this may have on the individual's drug misuse
- possible adverse social consequences such as job loss, problems with life insurance, home loans and housing.

If, after counselling, there are serious doubts about the individual's ability to cope with a positive result we consider it would not normally be to that person's advantage to have the test at that time. We see two exceptions to this general principle: where a test is necessary for differential diagnosis or where the individual is pregnant, or planning to become so, and risks giving birth to an infected baby.

5.23 Counselling about the antibody test is an important and difficult task. In the case of drug misusers it will usually be most effectively undertaken by staff who already know something about the individual and his or her drug use. All drug-specialist staff and general practitioners should therefore be trained to provide this counselling. Testing facilities should normally be available at specialist drug services. Where, exceptionally, this is not possible there should be a streamlined referral system to a local testing service.

5.24 We have heard evidence of a number of cases where drug misusers have been tested without their permission or without their knowledge and subsequently informed that they were antibody positive. We deplore this unprofessional behaviour and urge all professional bodies concerned to take action against any member who behaves in this way. There are also cases of drug misusers being refused admission to inpatient and residential rehabilitation facilities either because they refused to be tested or were known to antibody positive. We strongly disapprove of such practices and consider that they will do nothing to combat the spread of HIV and are likely to exacerbate the problem. In close communities, as in the community at large, successful prevention will depend upon educating individuals to regard everyone as potentially HIV positive and to take the necessary precautions.

5.25 **In conclusion, we recommend that antibody testing of individual clients should be used with caution and only undertaken with informed consent following full counselling (as outlined in para 5.22).** All drug-specialist staff and general practitioners should be equipped to provide this counselling and drug services should normally have the facilities to perform tests. Where testing cannot be done on site there should be a streamlined referral system for testing elsewhere. Being tested for HIV should never be a pre-condition of drug treatment or rehabilitation services.

Special Groups

5.26 Achieving behaviour change takes on even greater importance amongst drug misusers who are already infected with the virus, and amongst others who are at very high risk of acquiring and spreading it (e.g. prostitutes). The principles outlined in this report apply equally to such individuals. However, the risk they pose to the community generally, as well as to themselves, means that particularly intensive efforts may be needed to reach them and help them adopt safer practices. The wider question of management of HIV positive drug misusers will be addressed in our second report. Meanwhile, we cannot stress too strongly the need to maintain contact with them and to consider every possible way of helping each such individual move towards safer practices.

Drug Misusers who cannot be brought into contact with services

5.27 Although the changes we are recommending should enable services to make contact with much larger numbers of drug misusers, there will still be many drug misusers who remain out of contact with services. A major programme of information and education will be needed over a sustained period in order to reach this group. National campaigns will be of continued importance but local efforts are also necessary in all areas. Local publicity and education should give straightforward information about the risks of HIV and how to avoid them, availability of sterile injecting equipment, cleaning of equipment, safer sex, and the availability of services for drug misusers. A wide range of formats is likely to be most effective including, for example, posters and comics (but excluding excessively morbid presentations which are unlikely to be effective and may reinforce the misconception that people infected with HIV will look ill or abnormal). Efforts to make use of the grapevine and peer pressure will be as important as more formal approaches. Health Education Officers and Local

Education Authority Drug Co-ordinators will be well placed to make an important contribution to all this work which should, in our view, be co-ordinated by District Drug Advisory Committees. **We conclude that a campaign of education and information is needed both nationally and locally. In the long run we believe that sustained publicity and education will prove to be the most important influence on changing behaviour.**

5.28 A substantial number of injecting drug misusers, and those who might be tempted to inject, will not be in current contact, or even in contact at any time with services. Additionally, many episodes of injecting drug use are not planned, and occur in situations where there is no immediate access to new or clean equipment. These circumstances apply particularly to occasional injectors. It is vital therefore that drug misusers should know how to clean injecting equipment in the event that they do not have access to new equipment. **We recommend that advice on cleaning injecting equipment should be available in all areas. The advice should make clear that cleaning cannot offer full protection against infection and is no substitute for using clean equipment, but that it can help prevent infection when clean equipment is not available.**

6 Prescribing

6.1 This chapter discusses the role of prescribing in contributing to the twin functions of making and maintaining contact with drug misusers and changing their behaviour away from HIV risk practices. Our discussion illustrates the valuable contribution which prescribing can make but emphasises that it is not a panacea. In line with general principles laid down in the Guidelines of Good Clinical Practice[1], treatment, including prescribing, must be tailored to the individual drug misuser if it is to be as effective as possible in bringing about the desired changes.

Possible Purposes of Prescribing

6.2 In addition to the direct treatment function of assisting withdrawal from drugs, prescribing may serve two wider purposes directly related to our goal of containing the spread of HIV:

a. *Attracting more drug misusers to services and keeping them in contact*

Available evidence supports the view that a prescribing function in a drug service can be successful in attracting some drug misusers who would otherwise not approach services (or at least not do so until a later date). A recent study found that the vast majority of drug misusers interviewed would prefer a service which offered some form of pharmacological support. Of these, most favoured flexible arrangements rather than fixed options though the next most commonly mentioned option was a reducing prescription. Less than 20 per cent of the total sample (23 per cent of those not in contact with services) considered maintenance the ideal. We have also received anecdotal evidence of individual drug misusers taking drastic steps, such as moving house, to obtain treatment which included a prescription. Set against this, we note that many non-prescribing agencies are successful in attracting clients despite the proximity of a prescribing service. We

---

[1] Guidelines of Good Clinical Practice in the Treatment of Drug Misuse: Report of the Medical Working Group on Drug Dependence (DHSS, 1984).

conclude that prescribing is one of a number of factors which may attract drug misusers to services; for some it may be the most important, for others less important and for some it may be a deterrent. As with other aspects of service provision we consider that a range of approaches is necessary to attract the maximum number of drug misusers.

b. *Facilitating change away from HIV risk practices*

Research on the effect of prescribing in helping drug misusers towards abstinence is inconclusive. This is perhaps not surprising in view of the heterogeneity of drug misusers and the wide range of prescribing and other interventions which may be used. It is clear however that prescribing has helped some toward abstinence but has not helped, and has sometimes hindered others. But the advent of HIV means we must now address a different question; what role can prescribing play in moving drug misusers away from practices which can spread HIV? Here again there is no empirical research which enables direct comparison of prescribing and non-prescribing interventions and conclusive research may be impossible since drug misusers in either programme would be self, rather than randomly, selected. But there is evidence that the prescription of licit oral drugs to drug misusers is often associated with a reduction in their injecting of illicit drugs. There is also evidence that drug misusers in contact with prescribing agencies are less likely to share injecting equipment, though the role of prescribing in this is unclear. **We conclude that prescribing can be a useful tool in helping to change the behaviour of some drug misusers either towards abstinence or towards intermediate goals such as a reduction in injecting or sharing.**

Prescribing as a tool in fighting HIV

6.3 Para 5.2 identified the need for all interventions with drug misusers to recognise a hierarchy of goals and to work initially towards whichever goal or goals is most readily achievable. Once these 'intermediate' goals have been achieved efforts can focus on higher goals (ultimately abstinence) but great care must be taken with each individual not to prejudice what has already been achieved. For some drug misusers, prescribing will help attract them to treatment and improve the effectiveness of the treatment. In each such case, the purpose of prescribing should be clarified from the outset and the goals to be achieved identified by discussion/exploration with each drug misuser. The treatment given and the goals set should be individually tailored to the needs and circumstances of each drug misuser. In many

48

cases, it will be necessary to identify, and work towards, intermediate goals which fall short of abstinence. **Subject to our recommendation below about the levels at which prescribing should take place we recommend that the range of acceptable goals should include:**

a. **the cessation of sharing of equipment**
b. **the move from injectable to oral drug use**
c. **a decrease in drug misuse**
d. **abstinence.**

6.4 Having identified goals and decided upon treatment, it is most important that progress toward (or away from) these goals is monitored. If, over a reasonable time, the treatment being given is not resulting in progress towards the goals set then it must be reviewed and a new plan considered. This may include replacing outpatient prescribing with prescribing in an inpatient/residential setting, increasing involvement of third parties (e.g. family, drug-specialist or generic staff), or perhaps revising the agreed goals if they have been set too high. **No treatment package should continue indefinitely without review if it is failing to bring about, or sustain, a desirable change. This applies equally to non-prescribing interventions where review should include consideration of prescribing.**

6.5 Where intermediate goals are being achieved the object should be to set higher level goals following further discussion/explanation with the misuser and to monitor progress towards these.

Levels at which Prescribing Should be Undertaken

6.6 We have indicated above that different prescribing responses should be available to help different drug misusers towards a range of goals. In this section we discuss the levels of service at which these responses should be available. There is a clear analogy with other areas of health care: for example, GPs see it as within their remit to prescribe digoxin and propranolol to appropriate patients with heart disease, but require access to secondary level services for second opinions, investigations and the onward referral of more difficult cases.

6.7 In the same way, GPs should be equipped to deal with short-term detoxifications and medium term withdrawal regimes in co-operation where possible with Community Drug Teams or with support from voluntary sector drug agencies. More difficult cases may well require support from, or referral to local District specialist provision including Community Drug

Teams and the District psychiatrist with a special responsibility for drug misuse. The most difficult cases, such as those where non-reducing long-term prescriptions or the use of injectables is being considered, or where long-term inpatient treatment is needed, could appropriately be managed at District specialist level but may require referral to Regional Drug Problem Teams. It is important that specialist services should not become 'silted up' with cases which can be dealt with at a lower level.

6.8 Accordingly, we recommend that there should be a prescribing element to services in each District and Regional Drug Service which should undertake prescribing along the lines recommended in this report.

6.9 Assessing behaviour and behavioural change will be especially important in cases where prescribing is employed to aid the achievement of intermediate goals which fall short of abstinence (e.g. where the initial goal of treatment is that at para 6.3(a) or (b)). We recommend that wherever possible multi-disciplinary teams should be used in assessing and monitoring behaviour change.

Assessment Procedures for Prescribing

6.10 The need to minimise barriers to drug misusers seeking help and entering treatment is a theme which runs throughout this report. There is evidence of a significant drop-out rate amongst drug misusers who are required to undergo a lengthy assessment process (e.g. 1–2 weeks or longer) before active treatment is commenced. The advent of HIV makes it necessary to 'capture' many less well motivated misusers who are more likely still to be deterred by such a process. Equally, the prescribing of controlled drugs, with a high black-market value, in sizeable quantities to patients who have not been thoroughly assessed may exacerbate their drug problem and/or that of others. In turn it may lead to an increase, rather than a decrease, in shared injecting.

6.11 We therefore recommend that different assessment procedures should be introduced dependent on the anticipated treatment including the need for and length of, prescribing. Where prescribing is concerned, a balance must be struck between easy access to appropriate help and proper safeguards. Thus the assessment for a treatment response including time-limited oral methadone prescribing should be substantially shorter than that adopted before commencing longer-term prescribing or the prescribing of injectables. The effect of this recommendation should be to enable many patients to receive initial prescriptions sooner than they do at present.

Prescribing of Injectable Drugs and Non-opiates

6.12 In considering the role prescribing can play in attracting drug misusers to services and in changing behaviour towards a number of goals, it is not necessary or appropriate to discuss the fine detail of every prescribing option. However, it may be useful to explain how two particular types of prescribing fit into the framework we have described. First, prescribing of injectable drugs. Misuse of drugs by injection is particularly dangerous. It carries many risks in addition to that of acquiring and spreading HIV. Even where a drug injector regularly uses sterile equipment he or she may well share equipment on occasions when clean needles and syringes are not immediately to hand. A move from injecting drug use to oral use is therefore very desirable in cases where abstinence is not, for the time being, achievable. Much evidence indicates that such a move is achievable by large numbers of injecting drug misusers. This applies even to those who may have been attracted to clinics because they knew injectable drugs might be available. However, for some drug misusers a move away from injecting will not be achievable at the time they seek help (or consider seeking help). For these individuals the aim will be to:

a. move away from sharing equipment; and
b. provide treatment (in the broadest sense) which may facilitate a gradual change away from injecting use.

Clean equipment and education about safer practices will be required in all cases (see Chapter 5). In some cases, treatment which does not involve a prescription may help facilitate the gradual change from injecting use. In other cases, an oral prescription may facilitate gradual change in itself, may reduce the frequency of injecting drug misuse, and/or may be necessary to ensure the individual's continued participation in treatment thus keeping him/her exposed to therapeutic influence. In some cases – a small minority – prescribing of injectable drugs may be necessary to keep the individual in treatment and/or to ease the change from injecting the drug of dependence to taking a substitute orally. Where this is so, such prescribing of injectables should normally be undertaken for short periods only (rarely more than 3 months). The patient should understand from the outset that a change to oral use will be required, and that the injectable component of the prescription will reduce over time.

6.13 The prescribing of injectable drugs in this way will be an important element in helping some injecting drug misusers to move gradually away from injecting. Such cases will be exceptional. Prescribing injectable drugs carries greater risks than prescribing oral drugs and identifying and managing those cases in which it is necessary is a difficult and specialised task. Considerable safeguards will be required before such prescribing is undertaken and progress will need to be monitored very carefully. **We therefore recommend that cases in which prescribing of injectable drugs is being considered should be managed by, or with guidance from, the District or Regional specialist team.**

6.14 It has been argued that open-ended prescribing of injectable drugs could help to keep individuals who continue to inject drugs away from sharing equipment; so doing would keep the individual concerned in contact with a source of face-to-face health education and would reduce his/her need for contact with the black market (and perhaps with other injecting drug misusers).

However there are strong arguments against such an approach succeeding for the majority of drug misusers and wider practical arguments against such a policy:

- first, among the minority who may initially need to receive injectable drugs, most can be weaned on to oral substitutes within a reasonably short time;
- second, there is considerable evidence to show that a high proportion of drug misusers who receive prescribed injectable drugs continue to inject other drugs. These often include drugs which are not designed for injection and this can lead to greater physical damage and serious health problems;
- third, the long-term provision of injectable drugs may compound an individual's drug addiction, confirm his or her self-perception as a drug addict, thereby reinforcing a sense of hopelessness, and increase his or her drug tolerance;
- fourth, there is a potential risk of leakage into the black market of drugs with a high street value;
- fifth, individuals receiving injectable drugs need to be seen more frequently and may therefore rapidly silt up clinics, reducing or removing the clinics' ability to take on new clients.

6.15 In the light of these arguments **we recommend that only in the most exceptional case would long-term prescribing of injectable drugs be both necessary and effective in combating the spread of HIV. Any such cases**

should be managed by, or with guidance from, the Regional Drug Problem Team.

6.16 Finally we turn to the issue of prescribing for misusers of drugs other than opioids. In principle, the considerations discussed earlier in this chapter apply equally to such cases. There are however particular problems and risks associated with prescribing in these cases. Many misusers of amphetamines and other non-opioids are not heavy regular users and there is a serious danger that prescribing for them will increase their drug use leading in turn to greater instability. There is also a particular problem with prescribing drugs in tablet or capsule form which may subsequently be injected causing serious harm. **We recommend that in general, publicity and outreach combined with syringe exchange and advice and counselling services are the best means of reaching and influencing the behaviour of non-opioid misusers. There may however be very exceptional cases in which short-term prescribing of non-opioids might be helpful.**

7   AIDS and Drug Misuse in Scotland

Introduction

7.1 The conclusions and recommendations of this report apply to all parts of the UK. Nowhere is more urgent action needed to implement them than in Scotland where the problem of HIV infection in injecting drug misusers is especially severe. Yet services in Scotland are particularly ill-equipped to combat the spread of the virus. This situation pertains despite the report of the Scottish Committee on HIV infection and Intravenous Drug Misuse ('the McClelland Report'), published in September 1986, which recommended many sensible measures to combat the spread of the virus. We are deeply concerned that many of the report's recommendations have not been acted upon and we consider that valuable time has been lost in tackling the spread of HIV in Scotland.

7.2 This chapter examines aspects of the problem which are particular to Scotland and makes some additional recommendations for action there. In doing so we emphasise that many drug misusers are mobile and that failure to curb the spread of HIV in Scotland will inevitably lead to the virus spreading more rapidly throughout the UK and beyond. **HIV infection in Scottish drug misusers is not a problem for Scotland alone, it is a problem for the UK as a whole.**

7.3 It is now almost 3 years since surveys indicated a high prevalence of HIV infection in Scottish injecting drug misusers. Subsequent studies in Edinburgh and Dundee have confirmed prevalence rates of about 40–50 per cent in injecting drug misusers in the East of Scotland, suggesting a currently infected drugs misusing population there of 1100–1700. By contrast in the West of Scotland, rates of 2.5–5 per cent pertain albeit amongst a much larger pool of drug misusers. The latter is estimated at 5000 to 8000 strong with a total of about 200 to 400 infected. Thus in Scotland by October 1987, the proportion of injecting drug misusers amongst those known seropositives was 58 per cent (765) of a total pool of 1311. This contrasts starkly with England and Wales where only 7.5 per cent (470) of a total of 6246 seropositives were drug misusers. The youth of those affected is notable. Some 14.4 per cent (109) of those infected were under 20 years of age whilst 59 per cent (443) were under 25 years old. Of great significance for perinatal transmission, is the proportion – 34 per cent (257) – who are female, the overwhelming majority (90 per cent) being under 30 years old.

Special features of Drug Misuse in Scotland

7.4 Evidence indicates that many injecting drug misusers in Scotland are young and disadvantaged, often more so than their English counterparts. The greater proportion of younger injectors might be a consequence of the tendency in Scotland to begin experimental use of drugs by injection rather than inhalation. Whatever the reason, it makes many injecting drug misusers more difficult to contact through conventional services, especially those associated with authority and abstinence. There is also evidence of widespread misconceptions among them about HIV and its transmission. For example it may be believed that transmission occurs through use of heroin but not Temgesic or temazepam, or through needles but not syringes, or that healthy looking individuals will not be infectious.

7.5 Another feature of the drug problem in Scotland is that heroin has become scarce and of poorer quality and alternatives are being sought, leading to much greater poly-drug misuse. Of particular concern is the growing use of temazepam taken alone or injected in combination with heroin. This drug commonly produces serious behaviour disturbance with more chaos, violence and protracted memory blanks encountered.

Services for Drug Misusers in Scotland

7.6 There are four notable features of drug services in Scotland. First, the dearth of psychiatric input: psychiatrists in Scotland accept only a very limited role in the management of drug misusers and there is minimal specialist consultant provision in this field. As a result, advice and counselling agencies and the number of GPs who are prepared to work with drug misusers receive virtually no specialist support. This absence of back-up to help with the most problematical cases means that the energies of those in the front-line are all too easily sapped by small numbers of difficult clients with whom they are ill-equipped to deal. This, in turn, undoubtedly contributes to the unwillingness of many GPs to provide care and help for drug misusers.

7.7 Second, of the few doctors who are prepared to work with drug misusers only a handful are willing to consider the full range of treatment options including prescribing ones. This severely impairs the ability of services to make contact with drug misusers and to help them move away from HIV risk behaviour. It also means that these few doctors are overwhelmed with drug misusers and have to ration their use of prescribing in order to contain their workload. In practice this has led to the absurd position whereby treatment involving substitute prescribing is mostly available only to those already infected with HIV. Its use to prevent a seronegative drug misuser from engaging in HIV risk behaviour and acquiring the virus is virtually non-existent.

7.8 Third, major gaps remain in the provision of community-based services for drug misusers. In a proportion of existing agencies abstinence from drug misuse is the only goal and this emphasis does not attract drug misusers who are not yet motivated to give up. Whilst many agencies do some excellent harm-reduction work they are already severely overstretched.

7.9 Finally, the pilot syringe exchange schemes established in Scotland have been very different from most of the English schemes. In particular, they are hospital-based, medically supervised, have limited opening hours and can only issue up to 3 syringes at a time. They could hardly be described as 'user-friendly', and one is picketed by local residents. It is perhaps not surprising that they have failed to attract more than a tiny proportion of local injecting drug misusers.

Areas with High Prevalence of HIV infection

7.10 In areas of high seroprevalence, notably Edinburgh and Dundee, existing drug services are working under immense pressure. Advice and counselling services are having to deal with growing numbers of drug misusers and spend more time counselling each of them. The Edinburgh Infectious Diseases Unit is having to cope with the drug problems of seropositive patients as well as their HIV infection, and receives no psychiatric support in doing so. An attitude could be taken that, in these areas, infection is so widespread that energetic efforts to prevent further spread are doomed to failure because they are too late. Apart from justifying a sense of hopelessness in drug misusers and apathy in staff, this attitude misunderstands the nature of HIV infection in two important aspects. First there is evidence that continued injection of drugs stimulates infected lymphocytes to reproduce further virus and pushes the drug misuser towards AIDS which he/she may not otherwise have developed, or at least not so quickly. Secondly, there is evidence that as the immune system deteriorates then infectivity to others may rise dramatically. Therefore good management of infected drug misusers itself contributes to prevention. We will return to this issue in more depth in our Second Report.

Special Measures needed in Scotland

7.11 In addition to the measures recommended elsewhere in this report we make the following additional recommendations in respect of Scotland.

7.12 First, **all injecting drug misusers must have easy, uncomplicated access to advice on safer practices and to sterile injecting equipment.** The type of community-based service described at Annex C is urgently needed in Scotland. Although some existing community-based services in Scotland may be able to take on this role, new services will be needed in most cases. This is partly because existing services are thin on the ground and already overstretched and partly because some are too strongly associated with abstinence. The current pilot syringe exchange schemes will not provide a suitable base as they are inaccessible and unattractive to the vast majority of drug misusers. Even where existing services can be adapted, additional services will also be needed to bring provision overall up to the level necessary to make contact with the maximum number of drug misusers. These services should normally incorporate syringe exchange facilities but access to syringes through community pharmacies will also be needed (see para 5.17). This will be particularly important whilst syringe exchange facilities are in the process of being set up. Each Health Board should therefore hold immediate discussions with local pharmacists (or their representatives) to ensure that supplies are readily available in every district.

7.13 Second, **psychiatric input to the management and treatment of drug misuse is urgently needed.** General psychiatric services should provide treatment for drug misusers but psychiatric services specialising in drug misuse are also needed in areas where drug misuse is prevalent. **New full-time posts for consultant psychiatrists specialising in drug misuse need to be created in Glasgow and Edinburgh as a minimum.** They should be supported by multi-disciplinary teams as outlined in para 3.2(a).

7.14 Third, **the value of substitute prescribing, undertaken with care as outlined in Chapter 6, must be recognised.** The creation of specialist psychiatric services with a prescribing arm must be matched by an increased willingness at all levels to prescribe for drug misusers in appropriate cases.

7.15 Fourth, **local publicity and educational efforts (as outlined in para 5.27) will be especially important so as to get information to those drug misusers who are not in contact with services.** Intensive efforts will be necessary in Scotland in view of the youth and deprivation of many of those who must be reached.

7.16 Fifth, **Crisis Intervention Units should be developed in large cities to provide accommodation and care for injecting drug misusers at times of crisis.** This may be particularly important for HIV positive drug misusers, and increasingly necessary if the trend towards poly-drug use, with all its chaotic effects, continues.

7.17 Finally in view of the severity of the problem in Scotland it is essential that responsibilities are clearly defined, specific objectives are identified at all levels, and that progress towards these is closely monitored. This process must start at national level with the Scottish Home and Health Department and be mirrored at local level. Within each Health Board responsibility for planning, co-ordinating and monitoring measures to combat the spread of HIV through drug misuse should be specifically assigned to one individual, normally the most senior, the Chief Administrative Medical Officer. In exercising this responsibility the Medical Officer may wish to designate one or more appropriate and enthusiastic individuals, perhaps on a part-time basis, to assist him or her in implementing the measures proposed. In any case, the Medical Officer should seek advice from, and report regularly to, the Drug Liaison Committee.

8 AIDS and Drug Misuse in Prisons

The Significance of Prisons

8.1 The prison system is of major significance to our enquiry for a number of reasons. Large numbers of drug misusers spend some time in prison during their drug misusing career. Prison Department figures show that during 1986–87 3051 new inmates in England and Wales were found to have some degree of dependence on drugs. Other evidence suggests that the numbers are much larger: for example, a recent study of 121 drug misusers in London found that a quarter had been in prison during the past 12 months. Many drug misusers entering prison are likely to have injected, often with shared equipment, and growing numbers are likely to be HIV positive. Many of the women will have financed their drug misuse through prostitution.

8.2 Many drug misusers entering prison have had no previous contact with helping agencies. Almost all will find it much more difficult to obtain drugs inside prison. Many will therefore be at an appropriate point to reassess their drug misuse. Thus, prison represents a unique opportunity to reach large numbers of drug misusers for the first time, educate them towards safer practices and draw them into contact with a network of help that could reduce the risks to themselves and others.

8.3 Although prison is an artificial environment in which intentions cannot be fully tested, its potential to bring about sustained behaviour change is important. Efforts to achieve this are underlined by the need to minimise the risk of HIV transmission within prisons. Here, two special factors apply. First, although the scale of injecting drug misuse is likely to be minimal, if a syringe does get into the prison it is likely to be widely shared. Second, there is evidence to suggest that homosexual acts occur on a significant scale amongst male prisoners, including amongst some of those who are heterosexual when in the community.

61

8.4 We endorse the principle contained in the World Health Organisation consensus statement. 'Consultation on Prevention and Control of AIDS in Prisons' (November 1987) which reads, 'The general principles adopted by National AIDS Programmes should apply equally to prisons as to the general community'. The action necessary in prisons to combat the spread of HIV amongst drug misusers mirrors that required in the community generally i.e.

- prevent drug misuse wherever possible;
- maximise the number of drug misusers who are identified;
- work with each of them to encourage the adoption of safer practices (both while in prison and after discharge);
- educate those drug misusers who cannot be specifically identified, through publicity and general education for all inmates about HIV and safer practices.

Many of the conclusions and recommendations elsewhere in this report will apply either fully or particularly to prisons. In this Chapter we focus on some of the features and action peculiar to prisons.

Identification of Drug Misusers

8.5 Identification of drug misusers generally occurs on reception into prison when the new inmate is medically examined and asked to complete a questionnaire which includes questions about drug misuse. The rate of success in identifying drug misusers appears to be low (as illustrated in para 8.1). There are a number of factors which militate against successful identification:

a. medical officers on reception are required to deal with a large number of new prisoners in a short space of time. The medical examination is therefore likely to be fairly cursory in most cases;

b. the training of prison medical officers on drug misuse is patchy and many have little or no experience of working with drug misusers outside prison;

c. most drug misusers are likely to conceal their drug use as they fear stigmatisation including perhaps a discriminatory allocation policy and stricter security at visits and generally. Many may feel they have nothing to gain by declaring their drug misuse and plenty to lose;

d. the advent of HIV makes these problems more severe: identification of a history of injecting makes a prisoner liable to possible isolation and possible pressure to be tested for HIV antibodies.

8.6 Better training for prison medical officers – perhaps through short term attachments to specialist drug services in the community – will help in better identification. Spending more time with each prisoner on reception and conducting a more thorough medical examination is also important. This might be achieved through a revision of working practices or extra resources may be needed. But probably most important is providing incentives for drug misusers to come forward and minimising the deterrents for them to do so. Thus they need to believe that real help can be provided (including, where necessary, a short-term prescription to facilitate withdrawal), and that they will not suffer discriminatory treatment in any of the ways referred to above.

Treatment and Throughcare

8.7 The Prison Medical Service policy is that treatment to assist withdrawal from drugs is a matter for the individual clinical judgement of the prison medical officer concerned. We have heard evidence that practice differs significantly between prisons. Whilst withdrawal over 2–3 weeks using oral methadone appears to be fairly common in at least one prison, the use of methadone, or other drugs to control withdrawal symptoms, seems to be rare in other establishments. Abstinence in the short- (or fairly short-) term will normally be the appropriate goal in the special circumstances which prevail in prisons. But as elsewhere, the best treatment to bring about this goal should be selected from the full range of options. The prospect of a comfortable withdrawal from drugs may be the best incentive available to drug misusing prisoners to identify themselves.

8.8 Availability of advice and counselling within prisons remains patchy and we have detected no improvement compared to the position described in the Advisory Council's report of 1979. In respect of specialised therapeutic regimes, of the kind recommended in 1979, there has been a decrease. The evidence we have received suggests that, in some prisons at least, it has become more difficult in recent years for outside voluntary agencies to gain access. Against this background, we welcome the Prison Department's recent policy statement on throughcare of drug misusers in the prison system in England and Wales. The policy statement puts great emphasis on the work of the probation service. We have heard evidence of how overstretched the probation service is within prisons and of how little training and experience many seconded probation officers have in the field of drug misuse. A significant improvement in resources and training will be needed if the probation service is to fulfil its role.

Education about HIV

8.9 Controlling the spread of HIV in prisons, as in the community, depends largely on education to minimise risky behaviour. This applies both at a general level and an individual one, where one-to-one work may be necessary to educate a drug misuser away from risky practices. A good deal of effort has already gone into educating prison officers and other staff about AIDS and HIV and a video has been produced for them. We welcome this initiative as we consider it essential that prison staff be fully informed about HIV if they are to respond positively to the new demands it places upon them. Education on AIDS/HIV for prisoners still has a long way to go. We have been told that leaflets, such as the government leaflet 'AIDS – Don't Die of Ignorance' and the Health Information Trust's leaflet especially devised for prisoners, have been made available to prisons but we have heard evidence that distribution of leaflets within prisons has not always occurred. The Prison Department is currently considering the production of an educational video for inmates; we think such a video would make a useful contribution to formal education on AIDS/HIV and we hope it will be produced soon.

8.10 General education should be accompanied by the opportunity for private and confidential counselling on risk-reduction (as discussed in Chapter 5). Both general education and individual counselling should cover activities whilst in prison and following release. Thus education on heterosexual and mother to foetus transmission will be needed. The latter may be a potential problem in women already pregnant on admission to prison where there is a history of antecedent high-risk behaviour. We will address this in our second report. Similarly, education will need to cover the risks of injecting drug misuse and how they can be avoided, since some prisoners will return to drug misuse after release. It will also be important to recognise that homosexual acts do occur in prisons and to provide advice on the risks and how they can be avoided. Prison medical officers could in theory provide confidential advice on risk-reduction but we doubt that many prisoners would see this as a realistic option. We consider that outside agencies, usually in the voluntary sector, can play an important role as providers of this type of counselling and education and we recommend that the Prison Service should make full use of them as is indicated in the newly developed policy on throughcare for drug misusers. In order for this to develop satisfactorily opportunities for access by these agencies will need to be greatly improved.

Provision of Injecting Equipment and Condoms

8.11 The question of provision of injecting equipment in prisons is very different from that in the community generally. We have looked carefully at this issue but we cannot recommend the exchange or provision of equipment in prisons as a realistic option.

8.12 The Prison Department has argued that possession of condoms by prisoners cannot be allowed because it would condone homosexual acts. Such acts are regarded as unlawful in prison because nowhere within a prison can be deemed to constitute a private place. However, we have heard evidence that homosexual acts do occur in prisons to a significant extent. There are also indications that some men who are usually heterosexual engage in homosexual acts while in prison. Such activity, followed by a return to heterosexual activity after release could play an important role in spreading the virus amongst the heterosexual population. Thus, although such acts may be regarded as unlawful, it is clear that this does not stop them occurring.

8.13 The Government's forward-looking approach in setting up the pilot syringe exchange schemes provides a contrast to the approach of the Prison Department. Providing syringes in the general community does not condone illegal drug use. It is difficult to see how allowing access to condoms in prison could be regarded as condoning unlawful acts when placed within the context of the public health considerations involved. Clearly the safest course of action is for inmates to avoid anal intercourse but we have no doubt that, even with good health education, it will still occur to some extent. Use of condoms will offer some protection in these cases, though their effectiveness is limited. We note that a number of countries have recently decided to make condoms available in prisons. **We recommend that the Prison Department give urgent consideration to means of providing confidential but easy access to condoms.**

HIV Antibody Testing

8.14 We discussed the question of HIV antibody testing in Chapter 5 and urged that caution be exercised beforehand. The same considerations apply to testing in prisons. Even though chaotic drug use is unlikely to occur in a prisoner found antibody positive s/he may still suffer severe psychological effects. These in turn may have both short and long-term behavioural effects. Moreover, a prisoner who is known to be antibody positive may suffer stigmatisation and victimisation.

8.15 We therefore commend the Prison Medical Service's policy statement that testing should only be undertaken with consent and following counselling. Prison probation officers will often be best placed – because of their skills and relative independence – to provide such counselling and we consider that they should be given the necessary training. This counselling should involve a full explanation of how the individual will be allocated and treated in prison if found positive. It is important that prisoners are not rushed into having a test and particularly that testing should not be done at the time of reception. Counselling should be provided at two meetings with time for reflection in between.

8.16 Where a prisoner is known to be HIV positive he or she is placed under Viral Infectivity Restrictions (VIR). VIR was devised for inmates who were infected with Hepatitis B, which is far more infectious than HIV. We understand that Prison Medical Officers will decide, in the light of individual circumstances, which restrictions under the VIR headings are necessary in the care of someone who is HIV positive. Prison staff with an 'operational need to know' are informed of prisoners' VIR status. In practice this means that the confidentiality available to prisoners is rather limited. We appreciate the difficulties here but we hope that prison staff can be persuaded that in practice there will rarely be a 'need to know'. We are also concerned that the labelling of inmates in this way may result in inadequate health and safety precautions being taken with untested prisoners, who may of course be infected with the virus. We will return to the management of HIV positive drug misusers in prison in our Second Report.

Liaison with Community Services

8.17 The new emphasis on throughcare for drug misusers in Prison Department policy is welcome. It recognises the need for outside agencies to become involved with drug misusers who will be discharged into the district so as to provide them with support after release. In order to promote better liaison, District Drug Advisory Committees should have particular regard to the needs of prison populations and should develop links with local prisons. Regional Drug Advisory Committees should include in their membership a regional representative from the prison service.

Diversion from Prison

8.18 The problem of prison overcrowding is well known. The advent of HIV makes it even more undesirable that two or more prisoners should share a cell built for one with no toilet facilities. The possibility of homosexual acts in prison leading to HIV spreading in the heterosexual population means that every effort should be made to avoid imprisoning anyone who could adequately be dealt with in some alternative way.

8.19 Some drug misusers commit serious offences for which custody is an inevitable outcome. However, others are imprisoned for comparatively minor offences even though the relative ineffectiveness of such measures in preventing drug-related re-offending has long been recognised. We consider that increased use should be made of existing filters so as to minimise the numbers actually reaching prison, and especially to avoid unnecessary remands in custody. In particular, we consider that a more imaginative use of the probation order (with or without the condition of attendance at a day centre) would combine society's concern for the general problem with social work assistance to the individual. This in turn, would provide better opportunities than prison for risk-reduction advice to be given over a prolonged period. It would also produce greater hope of positive change with offenders being introduced to a range of alternative, more constructive, interests.

8.20 *In conclusion, we recommend that*:

a. **efforts to identify drug misusers in prison and to encourage them to identify themselves should be further increased;**

b. **further resources should be made available to enable the probation service to fulfil its role under the Prison Department's commendable new policy on throughcare;**

c. **urgent measures should be taken to improve the education of prisoners about HIV and risk-reduction. Full use should be made of outside agencies;**

d. **further consideration should be given to the possibility of prisoners being allowed easy confidential access to condoms;**

e. **District Drug Advisory Committees should have particular regard to the needs of prison populations and should develop links with local prisons. Regional Drug Advisory Committees should include in their membership a regional representative from the prison service;**

f. **increased use should be made of existing filters so as to minimise the number of drug misusers actually reaching prison and every effort should be made to avoid unnecessary remands in custody.**

9 Management, Organisation, Resources and Training

Management and Organisation

9.1 The advent of HIV and AIDS has many implications for the management and organisation of services. Those which arise directly from the specific recommendations we make about services will be self-evident and are not repeated here. We do, however, wish to highlight three themes which are important for those responsible for the management of services.

9.2 First, the need for very proactive and imaginative approaches in making contact with drug misusers. It will not be adequate simply to cater for existing 'demand'. A variety of ventures often using unproven techniques will be needed. A range of diverse approaches is likely to bring the maximum benefit.

9.3 Second, all services working with drug misusers need to recognise a hierarchy of goals (see Para 5.2), uppermost of which is that of combating the spread of HIV.

9.4 Third, the need to tackle HIV alongside drug misuse redoubles the importance of inter-agency working. This goes far beyond co-operation between those services primarily concerned with HIV/AIDS and those primarily concerned with drug misuse. Of key importance is the recognition that the services provided by a range of agencies working together is more likely to be effective in reaching many drug misusers and changing their behaviour than any single agency working in isolation. An increase in co-operative working between specialist and non-specialist agencies will be needed in many areas. Streamlined and effective referral procedures between agencies will be required. Many sections of the community will need to be informed and involved in the strategy to combat HIV amongst drug misusers.

9.5 We consider that Drug Advisory Committees provide the best forum for devising Regional and District strategies to tackle the spread of HIV through drug misuse. In some cases those committees will need to be strengthened to enable them play this role effectively. Cross-representation and close co-operation with AIDS Co-ordinating Committees (or their equivalent) will be essential. **We recommend that responsibility for monitoring and co-ordinating service provision to combat the spread of the virus through drug misuse should be clearly assigned to the District Medical Officer, who should seek advice from, and report regularly to, the District Drug Advisory Committee.**

Resources

9.6 Action to prevent the spread of HIV through drug misuse will inevitably cost money. Failure to take necessary preventive action will involve much greater future costs in both human and financial terms. The Introduction and Chapter 1 illustrated the speed with which the virus can spread through injecting drug misuse. We have also emphasised the potential importance of this route of transmission in introducing the virus to the general heterosexual population. There is no doubt that substantial investment in action to combat the spread of infection amongst drug misusers will prove to be many times cheaper than caring for the large number of cases of HIV infection and AIDS that will otherwise result.

9.7 Extra resources will be needed to implement our recommendations for two basic reasons. First, combating the spread of HIV requires that services reach and help more people. Second, the need to counsel about HIV and safer practices will require more time to be spent with each individual. No attempt has been made to quantify the extra resources needed but it will be clear that a substantial increase in the cash allocated to services for drug misusers will be required.

9.8 Central funding has been very effective in stimulating developments in both statutory and non-statutory services. It is encouraging that responsibility for a considerable number of such centrally funded projects has now been taken over by local funding authorities. But whether these projects will endure in the face of competition for resources remains to be seen. History would suggest that such funding in the drug misuse field will only last if there is both national and local support. It seems inescapable that when a special field of service is unpopular and may be near the bottom of any local priority list, serious consideration should be given to central funding or to funding devolved to health authorities which is separately earmarked and accounted for. We therefore welcome the Government's current policy of earmarking funds for drug misuse services. This policy should continue and extra cash made available for the implementation of our recommendations should also be earmarked. We are concerned that funding decisions for drug services have often been made for time-limited periods of 3 years or less. This can result in considerable stress for staff, impairing the efficiency of the service and creating difficulties in recruitment and retention. It can also result in staff effort being spent on seeking new sources of funds instead of providing a direct service to clients. Drug services will face tremendous demands over the coming years in tackling the HIV problem; they must not be handicapped by time-limited funding. Like any other service, they should be monitored and evaluated to assess their effectiveness and efficiency and to enable them to be further improved.

Training

9.9 HIV, and the recommendations we make on measures to combat its spread, have substantial implications for training of staff who come into contact with drug misusers. A number of opportunities exist for drug workers to receive training about AIDS. We have not attempted a comprehensive survey but the evidence suggests that such training is limited in scope and not universally available. Detailed recommendations about how training needs should be met will be addressed by a separate Working Group of the Advisory Council which is due to report shortly on training issues. We have however identified a number of training needs:

a. *For Drug-Specialist Staff and Prison Probation Officers*
   - basic training on AIDS and HIV and risk-reduction counselling (including, particularly, sexual counselling);
   - training on HIV antibody-test counselling;

b. *For General Practitioners*
   - as in (a) above, plus:
   - pre and post-qualification training on working with drug misusers;
   - continuing education for established GPs on a regular basis;
   - short-term attachments to specialist drug services (see para 4.11) (possibly including a short spell during vocational training for general practice);

c. *For Generic Workers (including GUM staff)*
   - as in (a) above, plus:
   - training on working with drug misusers;

d. *For Pharmacists*
  – basic training on drug misuse, AIDS/HIV and risk reduction;

e. *For Prison Medical Officers*
  – training on identifying and working with drug misusers.

We recommend that the relevant training bodies take steps to ensure that suitable arrangements for training are instituted as a matter of urgency. Health authorities should ensure that drug workers, including those from the voluntary sector, are not overlooked in arranging training on HIV/AIDS issues.

9.10 There will of course be many other training needs concerned with managing those drug users who become antibody positive. We will return to these in our second report.

10   Information and Research

10.1 Our enquiry has been assisted by a number of pieces of useful research to which we refer at the end of this report. However, it has also been hampered by a lack of information in a number of areas. We recognise that obtaining reliable information in the field of drug misuse can be difficult in view of the illicit nature of the activity. Moreover, information on behaviour, and factors which influence it, may be difficult to extrapolate from one group to another. Problems also exist in relation to information about HIV not least because most of those infected with the virus remain unidentified.

10.2 These difficulties make it all the more important that such information as is readily available should be properly recorded and collated. Yet many agencies which work with drug misusers do not keep even basic confidential records about client numbers and characteristics. In the absence of such records we find it hard to see how the effectiveness and efficiency of the service can be monitored and how future service developments can be planned. **We recommend that all agencies providing services for drug misusers should keep basic records which enable them to monitor the effectiveness of their work, particularly with regard to making contact with drug misusers and achieving behaviour change away from risky activities.**

10.3 Despite the difficulties outlined in para 10.1, useful research can be undertaken to supplement the information gained from the good record-keeping we advocate above. The following are priority areas for research into HIV and drug misuse:

a.   drug misusers who are not in touch with services (examining, for example, their awareness of HIV risk, their behaviour change, factors which influence their non-utilisation of services);
b.   factors involved in progression, or not, from non-injecting to injecting drug misuse;

c. the effectiveness of different treatment approaches in achieving risk-reduction;

d. the effectiveness of counselling in achieving risk-reduction;

e. the effectiveness of low threshold prescribing in attracting drug misusers and helping them achieve behaviour change.

10.4 Better information is also needed on the prevalence of HIV amongst drug misusers. Current information, which only covers those who have chosen to be tested, has obvious limitations. We hope it will be possible to undertake studies of groups which are not self-selected so as to provide more reliable epidemiological data. We re-emphasise that testing of individual clients or patients should only take place with their informed consent.

11 Summary of Conclusions and Recommendations

11.1 A summary of the main areas covered by the report and our conclusions on each are provided in the Overview at the start of the report.

11.2 Our detailed conclusions and recommendations are:

Basic Principles

1. The spread of HIV is a greater danger to individual and public health than drug misuse. Accordingly, we believe that services which aim to minimise HIV risk behaviour by all available means should take precedence in development plans. (2.1)

2. We must be prepared to work with those who continue to misuse drugs to help them reduce the risks involved in doing so, above all the risk of acquiring or spreading HIV. (2.2)

3. A change in professional and public attitudes to drug misuse is necessary as attitudes and policies which lead to drug misusers remaining hidden will impair the effectiveness of measures to combat the spread of HIV. (2.3)

4. Prevention of drug misuse is now more important than ever before and in the longer run the success or failure of efforts to prevent young people from embarking on a career of drug misuse will have a major effect on our ability to contain the spread of HIV. (2.5)

Service Provision

5. In all areas, substantial further expansion of drug misuse services will be necessary if services are to reach more drug misusers and play an effective role in curbing the spread of HIV. (3.10)

Maximising Contact with Drug Misusers

6. The advent of HIV requires an expansion of our definition of problem drug use to include any form of drug misuse which involves, or may lead to, the sharing of injecting equipment. This in turn means that services must now make contact with as many of the hidden population of drug misusers as possible. (4.3)

Community-Based Services

7. A pattern of community-based services should be available in each health district. (4.8)

75

General Practitioners

8. The advent of HIV makes it essential that all GPs should provide care and advice for drug misusing patients to help move them away from behaviour which may result in them acquiring and spreading the virus. Health authorities should ensure that appropriate support is available and that GPs are made aware of it. (4.10)

9. Clinical attachments by GPs to local specialist drug services should be actively encouraged. Short-term (e.g. 6–12 months) sessional contracts should be available to help build a pool of GPs with this experience. Wherever possible, their medical contribution should be provided with the support and advice of a consultant with special expertise in drug dependence. (4.11)

10. All doctors should receive some training at undergraduate and postgraduate level on the problem and management of drug misuse. Further training for GPs should also be provided at postgraduate level both during the three-year vocational training period and for established practitioners on a regular basis. (4.12)

Hospital-Based Specialist Services

11. If 'front-line' services are to be successful in making contact with more drug misusers the support available from hospital-based specialist services will need to be expanded and strengthened. Such support must be available in every District backed up by more specialist Regional support as outlined in the Treatment and Rehabilitation report. (4.16)

12. Hospital-based services should attempt to maximise contact with drug-misusers through: better dissemination of information about the service on offer; flexible opening hours; minimisation of waiting times. (4.17)

Generic Services

13. In the light of HIV, early identification and intervention by agencies which are not drug-orientated but which nonetheless come into contact with large numbers of drug misusers is of heightened importance. (4.18)

14. If drug misusing parents are not to be deterred from seeking help, Social Services Departments should work hard to ensure that drug misuse *per se* is never, and is never seen as, a reason for separating parent and child. (4.20)

15. Drug services should experiment with a variety of approaches to outreach work and monitor carefully their effectiveness in reaching drug misusers not in touch with services, and in conveying help and advice. (4.29)

Changing Behaviour

16. All services in contact with drug misusers should inform them of the risks of HIV and how they can avoid and reduce these risks both sexual and of injecting. (5.9)

17. All services for drug misusers, including general practitioners, should have the facility to provide free condoms. (5.10)

18. Further syringe exchange schemes should be set up drawing on the experience of the more successful pilot projects. Monitoring of these schemes should continue so that their success in reaching drug misusers and changing their behaviour can be assessed. We emphasise, however, that for some drug

misusers behaviour change may take several months to occur and these schemes should not be judged wholly by short-term results. Ultimately they must be judged on lasting evidence of behaviour change. (5.16).

19. Community pharmacists should be encouraged to sell equipment at reasonable cost to injecting drug misusers, and, wherever possible, pharmacists should advise customers about any local exchange facility, encourage the use of condoms, and provide health education and information on local facilities for drug misusers by provision of leaflets and, where possible, by verbal advice. Health authorities should provide pharmacists, on request and free of charge, with disposal facilities for used equipment and pharmacists should encourage customers to return used equipment. (5.17)

20. All syringes should bear an indelible warning about the danger of sharing injecting equipment. The Government should discuss with syringe manufacturers how this can be achieved as soon as possible. (5.18)

21. District Drug Advisory Committees and Local Pharmaceutical Committees should immediately agree a plan for ensuring and advertising the availability of injecting equipment in the light of local circumstances. Local police should be consulted on and should co-operate with the agreed plan, to ensure that police activity does not discourage drug misusers from obtaining sterile equipment and/or returning equipment. (5.19)

22. Antibody testing should be used with caution and only undertaken with informed consent following full counselling. All drug-specialist staff and general practitioners should be equipped to provide this counselling and drug services should normally have the facilities to perform tests. Where testing cannot be done on site there should be a streamlined referral system for testing elsewhere. Being tested for HIV should never be a pre-condition of drug treatment or rehabilitation services. (5.25)

23. A campaign of education and information is needed both nationally and locally. In the long run we believe that sustained publicity and education will prove to be the most important influence on changing behaviour. (5.27)

24. Advice on cleaning injecting equipment should be available in all areas. The advice should make clear that cleaning cannot offer full protection against infection and is no substitute for using clean equipment, but that it can help prevent infection when clean equipment is not available. (5.28)

Prescribing

25. Prescribing can be a useful tool in helping to change the behaviour of some drug misusers either towards abstinence or towards intermediate goals such as a reduction in injecting or sharing. (6.2)

26. Subject to our comments about the levels at which prescribing should take place, the range of acceptable goals towards which drug misusers might move with the help of prescribed drugs should include:

    a.   the cessation of sharing of equipment;
    b.   the move from injectable to oral drug use;
    c.   decrease in drug misuse;
    d.   abstinence. (6.3)

27. No treatment package should continue indefinitely without review if it is failing to bring about, or sustain, a desirable change. This applies equally to non-prescribing interventions where review should include consideration of prescribing. (6.4)

28. There should be a prescribing element to services in each District and Regional Drug Service which should undertake prescribing along the lines recommended in this report. (6.8)

29. Assessing behaviour and behavioural change will be especially important in cases where prescribing is employed to aid the achievement of intermediate goals which fall short of abstinence. We recommend that wherever possible multi-disciplinary teams should be used in assessing and monitoring behaviour change. (6.9)

30. Different assessment procedures should be introduced dependent on the anticipated treatment including the need for, and length of, prescribing. Where prescribing is concerned, a balance must be struck between easy access to appropriate help and proper safeguards. (6.11)

31. Cases in which prescribing of injectable drugs are being considered should be managed by, or with guidance from, the District or Regional specialist team. (6.13)

32. Only in the most exceptional case would long-term prescribing of injectable drugs be both necessary and effective in combating the spread of HIV. Any such cases should be managed by, or with guidance from, the Regional Drug Problem Team. (6.15)

33. In general, publicity and outreach combined with syringe exchange and advice and counselling services are the best means of reaching and influencing the behaviour of non-opioid misusers. There may however be very exceptional cases in which short-term prescribing of non-opioids might be helpful. (6.16)

AIDS and Drug Misuse in Scotland

34. HIV infection in Scottish drug misusers is not a problem for Scotland alone, it is a problem for the UK as a whole. (7.2)

35. All injecting drug misusers must have easy, uncomplicated access to advice on safer practices and to sterile injecting equipment. (7.12)

36. Psychiatric input to the management and treatment of drug misuse is urgently needed. New full-time posts for consultant psychiatrists specialising in drug misuse need to be created in Glasgow and Edinburgh as a minimum. (7.13)

37. The value of substitute prescribing, undertaken with care, must be recognised. (7.14)

38. Local publicity and educational efforts will be especially important so as to get information to those drug misusers who are not in contact with services. (7.15)

39. Crisis Intervention Units should be developed in large cities to provide accommodation and care for injecting drug misusers at times of crisis. (7.16).

AIDS and Drug Misuse in Prison

40. Efforts to identify drug misusers in prison and to encourage them to identify themselves should be further increased. (8.20)

41. Further resources should be made available to enable the probation service to fulfill its role under the Prison Department's commendable new policy on throughcare. (8.20)

42. Urgent measures should be taken to improve the education of prisoners about HIV and risk-reduction. Full use should be made of outside agencies. (8.20)

43. Further consideration should be given to the possibility of prisoners being allowed confidential access to condoms. (8.20)

44. District Drug Advisory Committees should have particular regard to the needs of prison populations and should develop links with local prisons. Regional Drug Advisory Committees should include in their membership a regional representative from the prison service. (8.20)

45. Increased use should be made of existing filters so as to minimise the number of drug misusers actually reaching prison and every effort should be made to avoid unnecessary remands in custody. (8.20)

Management, Organisation, Resources and Training

46. Responsibility for monitoring and co-ordinating service provision to combat the spread of the virus through drug misuse should be clearly assigned to the District Medical Officer who should seek advice from, and report regularly to, the District Drug Advisory Committee. (9.5)

47. The relevant training bodies should take steps to ensure that suitable arrangements for training are instituted as a matter of urgency. Health authorities should ensure that drug workers, including those from the voluntary sector, are not overlooked in arranging training on HIV/AIDS issues. (9.9)

Research

48. All agencies providing services for drug misusers should keep basic records which enable them to monitor the effectiveness of their work, particularly with regard to making contact with drug misusers and achieving behaviour change away from risky activities. (10.2).

Advisory Council on the Misuse of Drugs

Working Group on AIDS and Drug Misuse

Members

Chairman: **Mrs R Runciman** – Citizens Advice Bureau, Hackney.

Mr H Goodwin – Project leader, West Edinburgh Support Team.

Dr D Hawkins BSc MRCP – Consultant Physician in Genito-Urinary Medicine and Venereology, St Stephens Hospital, Fulham, London.

Mr M Hindson B Soc Sci – Assistant Chief Probation Officer, Greater Manchester Probation Service.

Dr M Keen MB BCh DPM – Consultant Psychiatrist, Adfer Addiction Unit, Cardiff.

Dr D Kennedy MB ChB MRCP D Obst RCOG – Consultant Physician, Ruchill Hospital, Glasgow.

Mr M Poling – Nurse Adviser to the Wessex Regional Drug Problem Team.

Mr C Smart – Director of Social Services for South Tyneside.

Dr G Stimson BSc MSc PhD – Researcher, Goldsmiths' College, London.

Dr J Strang MRCPsych – Consultant Psychiatrist, Drug Dependence Clinical Research and Treatment Unit, The Maudsley Hospital, London.

Dr A Thorley MA MB BCHIR FRCPsych – Consultant Psychiatrist, Parkwood House Alcohol and Drug Problem Service, Newcastle-upon-Tyne.

Mr D Turner – Director, Standing Conference on Drug Abuse.

Dr T Waller MB BS MRCS LRCP – General Practitioner, North London.

As Chairman of the Council **Dr P H Connell** CBE FRCP MD FRCPsych DPM is an ex-officio member of the Group.

Secretary:	Mr A Woods
Assisted by:	Mr J Morgan
	Ms P Parris

Officials

Department of Health and Social Security

Mrs E Shaw (succeeded by Mr W Burroughs from October 1987)
Dr D Black
Ms S Bateman

Home Office

Mr D Cooke (succeeded by Mr R Hazell from September 1987)

Scottish Home and Health Department

Mr J Gilmour
Dr R Melville

Northern Ireland Office

Dr P McClements

Welsh Office

Mr D Jennings

Terms of Reference

To examine the implications of AIDS for drug misuse services and report urgently on measures which can be taken by services to help combat the spread of HIV infection. In particular, to report on action which can be taken to:

a. provide more drug users with the opportunity of contact with appropriate helping services.
b. to help to keep people who continue to misuse drugs in contact with treatment or other appropriate services with a view to preventing or minimising unsafe injecting and other harmful behaviour.
c. to examine and report upon the wider implications of AIDS and HIV for all services for drug misusers including the provision of treatment and other services to drug misusers who have HIV infection or AIDS or may be at risk.

Evidence Submitted to the Working Group

During the first part of its enquiry the Working Group has received evidence, both oral and written, from a wide range of individuals and bodies. Those who provided evidence included:

Consultant Physicians
Consultant Psychiatrists
Nurses
Social Workers
Probation Officers
Police Officers
Prison Medical Officers
A Prison Psychologist
A Prison Hospital Officer
General Practitioners
Community Pharmacists
Health Authority Managers
Directors of Social Services/Social Work
Researchers
Staff from genito-urinary medicine clinics
Staff from drug advice and counselling services (statutory and non-statutory)
Staff from syringe exchange schemes
A Youth Worker
Staff from residential rehabilitation services
Staff from AIDS counselling and advice services
A detached drugs worker
A private medical practitioner

Annex C

Development of Community-Based Services

Objective of Service

1 To contact drug misusers and help them to minimise the risk and damage to themselves and others as a result of their drug misuse. In particular, to provide advice and help in reducing the risk of acquiring and transmitting HIV by whichever means are most readily achievable by each individual concerned.

Service Base and Access

2 The service should be based in a location which is easily reached by the local drug misusing population. A town centre location will often be ideal though a side street will probably be preferable to a main street since it will be important that people using the service do not feel conspicuous. In some districts more than one base will be necessary to ensure that the service is accessible to the whole population.

3 In rural areas with poor public transport the use of a mobile unit may be one way of reaching the population. Similarly, in urban areas where particular estates or districts are known to have many drug misusers a mobile unit visiting each estate may be a worthwhile approach. It should be borne in mind, however, that if such units are unduly conspicuous they may be unattractive to many drug misusers who would prefer a discreet service. An alternative would be for the staff of the service to work from a number of static bases such as advice centres, health centres etc. In some cases, a flat (or house) in a 'problem' estate may provide an ideal base. Where a mobile unit is used it will generally be preferable for it to be linked with a stationary base.

4 Opening hours should be tailored, as far as possible, to the needs and habits of drug misusers. This will often mean evening opening (perhaps in place of mornings), perhaps including weekends. This should fit in better

with the daily pattern of many drug misusers' lives; it will also provide easier access for those who are working.

5 Immediate access is extremely important since drug misusers who are not highly motivated may not be willing to wait or return if they can not be seen straight away.

Staffing and Style of Service

6 The service should be perceived as practical, non-judgemental, informal and geared to the user's needs and problems. Former drug misusers may be particularly effective in this role. In the past, the voluntary sector has often been in the forefront of this type of service development. Its role will remain important but, as Community Drug Teams have demonstrated, it is possible to provide this type of service very well in the statutory sector. Either way, care must be taken to avoid over-identification with 'authority'.

7 Some professional input will be required on a 'consultancy' basis. This may be from sessional GPs (to provide primary health care and, where required, help with drug problems), and advisers to help with non-drug problems.

Service Provided

8 The service provided must be geared both to achieving the objectives in para 1 above and meeting the needs of drug misusers so they find it relevant and attractive. The provision of help and advice which is not directly related to drug misuse may be the 'carrot' which persuades many drug misusers to make and maintain contact. The service on offer should therefore include:

a. *Practical advice and help*
In particular, advice and help with the type of problems which drug misusers often suffer but are not directly related to their drug use. Examples include welfare benefit advice, housing and employment advice, help with child care and legal problems. The staff of the service should be able to provide some advice and help of this sort but will also need to call on others with more expertise. In some cases it may be useful for outside staff with expertise in one of these fields to do a periodic advice session at the service (staff from the LA housing emergency department, the Manpower Services Commission, a legal advice centre, are obvious examples). An alternative would be for the staff of the service to develop a network of contacts who

could advise them (usually by telephone) on individual cases. At a still more practical level, the provision of facilities such as launderettes and creches may be effective in attracting clients. This kind of practical help not only meets clients' needs but may also enable them to attend the service without feeling stigmatised.

b. *Advice or help on HIV and how to avoid it*
The advice given must recognise that some drug misusers are not yet sufficiently motivated to consider abstinence and that others are not yet ready to stop injecting. All clients must be given non-judgemental practical advice about the different ways of avoiding acquiring or transmitting the virus. This is discussed in more detail in Chapter 5. The provision of condoms and syringe exchange will reinforce the health education and provide the means to put it into practice. This should normally be part of the service though provision of syringe exchange is not essential providing there are other outlets locally. Where this is the case, advice on where to obtain syringes should be readily available.

c. *General medical care*
Many drug misusers do not have general practitioners and are often in need of primary health care. A general practitioner or hospital doctor should normally be employed by the service on a sessional basis to provide treatment for problems such as abscesses and other illnesses together with family planning and cervical cytology. If this is not possible, the service should develop links with local GPs who are willing to deal with referrals. Advice and support in getting a GP should be available.

d. *Help with drug problems*
Help with drug problems should be available for those who want it. The permanent staff should be trained and equipped to provide advice and counselling. More specialist help, including the possibility of prescribing, may be provided in a variety of different ways e.g:

- through the sessional GP, or in liaison with the client's own GP;
- through specialist drug staff (e.g. community psychiatric nurses) attached full- or part-time to the service (again, in liaison with a GP or hospital-based specialist);
- by referral to the local drug dependency unit.

Advertising and Outreach

9 The services should be extensively advertised. Advertising should spell out clearly what services are on offer rather than just publishing the

existence of the service. It should make it clear to drug misusers that the services are for them but that they are not only about drug misuse. It must also be made clear that the services are not only for those who feel motivated to stop or reduce their drug misuse. The health and practical advice aspects of the services should be highlighted. Suitable sites for advertisements may include retail pharmacies, accident and emergency departments, GPs' surgeries, youth organisations, launderettes, 'take-aways'.

10 Some of these services, e.g. mobile units, will be a form of 'outreach' in themselves. More generally, all the services should form a useful base for outreach work where this is considered appropriate.

Links with other services

11 Good links and easy two-way referral will be essential with:

- other drug counselling/advice services;
- local GPs;
- drug dependency units (or other specialist psychiatric services where there is no DDU);
- GUM clinics;
- residential rehabilitation services;
- social services;
- other statutory services such as housing departments, social security offices, the Manpower Services Commission;
- other (non-drug) advice agencies.

Figure 1 The changing nature of drug services and prevention work in the light of HIV and drug misuse.

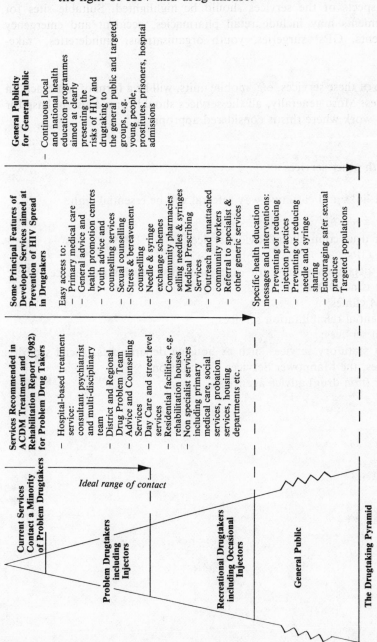

A problem drugtaker is defined in the T & Rehab Report as any person who experiences social, psychological, physical or legal problems related to intoxication and/or regular excessive consumption and/or dependence as a consequence of his own use of drugs or other chemical substances (excluding alcohol and tobacco).

89

Services for Drug misusers in England

A Paper by DHSS

Introduction

1 This paper attempts to assess the level of services currently available for drug misusers. It is based on the latest factual information available in the Department, namely:

a. information gathered from Regions' out-turn reports for 1986–87;

b. other centrally available statistics;

b. data from the interim report by Birkbeck College of their evaluation of services developed as a result of the Central Funding Initiative.

Centrally Available Statistics

2 Health Service statistics available from the specialist facilities return for 1986 show that there are currently 11 drug dependence units in England, and six drug and alcohol units containing 127 and 125 beds respectively. There are no statistics for undesignated beds in the general health service units which are available.

3 There are 36 residential rehabilitation facilities in England at present. This figure includes those run by both the voluntary and private sectors.

Information from Regions' out-turn reports

4 Regional Health Authorities submit annual out-turn reports to the Department on the development of hospital and community health services over the previous year. Scrutiny of Regions' out-turn reports for 1986–87 has just been completed. In order that the responses from Regions should be as uniform as possible, we asked that the out-turn reports include answers for drug misuse services within each Region and District. In

addition to questions about new developments started during 1986–87 and whether they were the result of joint planning with other service providers, Regions were asked specifically:
- Is there a multi-disciplinary Drug Advisory Committee in every District?
- Within the Region, is there:
  - a specialist treatment facility;
  - access to specialist advice for professionals;
  - long-term residential accommodation?
- Within each District, are there:
  - access to advice and counselling;
  - psychiatric services and in-patient beds;
  - laboratory facilities?

Details of Regional out-turns

5 With only one exception, every district now has a Drug Advisory Committee, and the majority have wide representation including the health service, primary care, social services, the voluntary sector, education, housing, probation, and the police.

6 All Regions state that they provide access to specialist treatment facilities and specialist advice for professionals, although in one or two Regions centres are inconveniently placed and limited in scope.

7 The provision of residential rehabilitation remains patchy, with some Regions relatively well provided (Wessex) and two (West Midlands and North East Thames) without any long-term residential rehabilitation at all. Provision is almost entirely within the voluntary sector and growth has therefore been unplanned. Until the developments of the last few years (resulting largely from the Central Funding Initiative), residential rehabilitation facilities were concentrated in the south-east, but geographical distribution has now evened out, although until two units planned for the West Midlands open, there will remain no provision between Oxford and Sheffield. Facilities for women with children remain limited: only half a dozen units exist or are planned within the next few years.

8 There has been rapid development in advice and counselling services in the last few years, and these are now available to some extent in all Districts, often provided by the voluntary sector. It is noticeable that it is in this area

that most progress has been made, possibly because these services are less costly and complicated to set up than, for instance, residential facilities.

9 About two-thirds of Districts have access to psychiatric services and in-patient beds for drug misusers within the District. However, in some cases these facilities are not as accessible or as extensive as they might be, and it is difficult to assess the quality of the service offered. In a significant number of Districts which report having treatment facilities within the District, there is no consultant with a special interest in drug misuse, and ready access to in-patient beds is also uncertain. It may be that some Districts represent their general psychiatric services as being the formal back-up.

10 The provision of district-based laboratory facilities appears available in all Regions. However, one Region has cited the high cost of district-based laboratory facilities which also meet the safety requirements for the protection of HIV infection as a reason why such services rely on the Regional laboratory service.

General observations

11 Approximately 200 separate developments have been indentified from these out-turn reports, the majority funded from the £5m special allocation for drug misuse services made to health authorities in 1986–87. This means that approximately one new service development was funded for each District in England in 1986–87, the first year in which the extra £5m was made available to health authorities. Of course, the size and scope of these projects varies enormously, from the appointment of a community psychiatric nurse to funding for an entire Drug Problem team, or contributions to the funding costs of a voluntary organisation providing residential accommodation. However, it provides an indication of the extent of development of services facilitated largely by the additional £5m.

12 The spread of services is also still rather patchy with gaps where little appears to be developing, often as a result of individual Districts' views that they do not have a drug misuse problem.

13 The picture across the country on joint planning with Social Services remains unsatisfactory, six Regions showing little or no evidence of this in their plans.

14 In summary, there has been progress in the level of services provided by Districts but there remains some inconsistency across the country. Regions need to continue to monitor and stimulate those districts which do not provide accessible facilities for drug misusers. These shortcomings are being followed up with Regions either directly or through the review processes.

The Central Funding Initiative

15 The Government set up the Central Funding Initiative in 1983 to pump-prime the development of local services. All the funds available under the Initiative have now been fully committed. £17.5 million has been allocated to 188 local projects. The Department has commissioned a research project from Birkbeck College examining the impact of the CFI on service provision. The project has recently published an interim report, and some interesting and positive data has emerged. Although the data relates only to projects funded under the Initiative, these constitute a substantial proportion of recent service development, and the report provides a useful picture of recently developed provision.

16 There has been significant development of the voluntary sector under the Initiative – voluntary projects constituted 42 per cent of those funded.

17 Almost half the funding went to community-based services and half the projects funded (in money terms) constituted new services, as opposed to extensions of existing ones.

18 One of the indicators of the demand for and appropriateness of the projects funded under the CFI is the extent to which statutory authorities are prepared to pick up the funding for these projects once central funding ends after the maximum of three years. At the time of the research team's interim report, information on 29 of the first 35 projects whose funding had ended was obtained. It is encouraging that all but two projects had either secured future funding or were still negotiating with potential funders. Of the two which were not continuing, one had been an information-gathering exercise and was therefore not appropriate for ongoing funding, and the other, while not continuing in its present form, was under consideration by the DHA as a permanent service from this year.

19 The report indicates that 54 per cent of clients from projects studied in detail were women. This is an interesting finding, and reinforces the need for services to be aware of women drug users' particular needs.

20 Of the factors that caused projects to change their objectives since they were first set up, issues surrounding HIV infection were most prominent.

Services for Drug Misusers in Scotland

A Paper by the Scottish Office (Abridged Version)

1 Service Provision – General

1.1 The provision of primary medical care and hospital services for the treatment of drug misusers under the NHS is the responsibility of Health Boards who are expected to determine the level of hospital and community-based specialist services to be provided in their areas in the light of their assessment of local needs, taking account of national guidance. Drug misusers may receive treatment from general practitioners, hospital or community-based services or doctors in private practice. Non-emergency hospital services for drug misusers have hitherto been provided in Scotland in mental hospitals or psychiatric units of general hospitals. Only two hospital-based services specifically for drug misusers are in operation in Scotland.

1.2 The rehabilitation of drug misusers and their re-integration into society, which is an essential part of treatment, may be undertaken by local authority social work departments, by the Health Service or by voluntary bodies. Local authorities do not have specific powers or duties in relation to drug misuse but may provide services, including residential accommodation, in terms of their general powers under the Social Work (Scotland) Act 1968. In practice, outwith Strathclyde Region, existing rehabilitation services for drug misusers are provided mainly by voluntary organisations often with support from local authority or NHS personnel. In Strathclyde, the social work department has placed special emphasis on the planned provision of services for drug misusers and has developed a range of community-based services.

1.3 Prior to 1983 – 84 services for drug misusers in Scotland (other than hospital-based services) were almost non-existent; but a range of community-based services has developed rapidly in the last three to four years from this low base. The Register of Helping Agencies published by the Scottish Health Education Group (third edition, August 1987) contains a full list of the services available in Scotland.

2 Grants to assist Local Initiatives

2.1 To assist and encourage the development of services for drug misusers the Scottish Home and Health Department established with effect from 1984–85 a scheme of three-year grants to support local initiatives by Health Boards, local authorities and voluntary bodies. Additional support was provided by the Social Work Services Group by way of three-year pump-priming grants under section 10 of the Social Work (Scotland) Act 1968. Some 26 projects have received support under these programmes. The selection of projects for funding was made on the basis of three main criteria: resources should be directed to areas of widespread drug misuse; the desirability of funding a range of projects with a view to future evaluation; and the need to increase the provision of community-based projects.

2.2 Monitoring of the centrally-funded projects was undertaken on a model known as 'implementation monitoring' which was designed to assess in a systematic way how well each project was achieving the objectives which it had set itself. The evaluation covered all aspects of the projects work including objectives, organisation, management, methods used and staff training. It also assessed the status of each project within its local community and the identity which it had established; but it did not attempt to measure the performance of the project in terms of client outcome in view of the many variables involved and the relatively short period for which the projects had been in operation.

2.3 With one or two exceptions the projects were found to be well-managed with clear lines of responsibility and good support systems for workers. Overall, the community-based projects were judged to have made a significant contribution to combating drug misuse through the direct provision of services to drug misusers and their families and through informing the local communities about the problems of drug misuse.

3 Future Planning of Services

3.1 The need to develop services quickly in response to a rapidly-increasing drug problem and the use of short-term central government funding (as originally announced) to meet this need meant that little effort was devoted to forward planning which now needs to be addressed. In addition to service provision, training needs should be identified and met.

3.2 In February 1987 SHHD issued a Circular which set out detailed arrangements under which Health Boards would assume responsibility from 1 April 1987 for the administration of the local projects previously funded by SHHD. In order to provide continuity and a more secure financial base for managers and staff, particularly in voluntary projects, the arrangements provided that projects would be funded for at least a further three years from 1987–88 up to a maximum of seven years, subject to evaluation. Copies of the evaluation reports produced on each project by the Scottish Office (see section 2 above) were sent to the Health Boards concerned. Health Boards are now required to monitor the performance of these projects in consultation with the local authority social work department as appropriate.

3.3 Local drug projects, particularly those run by voluntary bodies, have tended to feel detached and isolated from the usual processes of local service planning and provision by Health Boards and local authorities. The new arrangements for the administration of projects by Health Boards are intended as an integral part of the range of services for which they are responsible. In this connection there are encouraging signs in several areas that local drug liaison committees are becoming increasingly involved in the detailed planning and provision of services.

4 HIV Infection and the need to expand Drug Misuse Services

4.1 The Circular issued in February 1987 also invited Health Boards to co-ordinate local proposals and apply to the Department for an allocation of funds for the expansion of services for drug misusers. Counselling about HIV infection and the risk of AIDS is now an integral part of the work of drug misuse services throughout Scotland but particularly in Edinburgh, Dundee and Glasgow. Discussion with drugs workers suggests that the counselling time required for each client (including the families and friends of misusers) as a result of the AIDS problem has increased by as much as 50 per cent. An extra £300,000 per annum is being made available from 1987–88 under this support programme, bringing the total set aside in the Health programme specifically for the support of drug misuse services to over £1m per annum. The Circular made clear that one of the factors taken into account in deciding to increase the resources available under this programme was the need for these services to provide information, advice and counselling about HIV infection for drug misusers and their families and friends; and proposals for new initiatives would be expected to take account of this need.

4.2 In considering individual proposals and determining the allocations to Boards, the Department reviewed the pattern of existing services and took into account available information about the incidence of drug misuse, in particular by injecting, and the areas where the main concentrations are of people at risk of contracting or transmitting HIV infection through injecting drug misuse. We concluded that in view of the scale of the drugs and HIV infection problem in Edinburgh, Glasgow and Dundee and the very heavy pressure on the existing drug misuse services in these areas, the allocation of funds should be confined to proposals in these areas. We discussed the proposals from these areas with the Health Boards and local authorities concerned and agreed with their view that priority should be given to strengthening or expanding the range of existing services rather than establishing new projects.

4.3 The Department's scrutiny of the proposals submitted by Boards indicates that some gaps in the services provided – in geographical terms and the type of services available – will remain. In particular there were several proposals from Glasgow and one or two other parts of Strathclyde Region and from Lothian, Central and Grampian Regions which we considered worthy of support but which did not merit a higher priority than those accepted for funding. We hope that Health Boards and local authorities will explore other ways in which these proposals might be funded.

4.4 *Training*

In addition to the additional funds being allocated to the three Health Boards we are increasing substantially our support for the Drugs Training Project at Stirling University to enable it to recruit two additional training organisers. This is one of the most important and most successful of the local initiatives to which we gave grant support in 1984. The project's original remit was to provide training for drugs workers and volunteers in the new local projects and for staff in social work departments. As the number of local projects has grown and in-service training programmes for teachers, community education workers and other professional groups have been developed, the role of the Stirling project has developed to the point where it is effectively a national drugs training centre providing training and training advice for a wide range of bodies. HIV infection and AIDS have also added a major new dimension to drug-related training. The expansion of local services will also add to the project's workload so we see the expansion of the drugs training project as an essential part of the development of these services.

4.5 SHHD is also providing support for three years for an additional lecturer post at the Alcohol Studies Centre at Paisley College of Technology to concentrate on the provision of in-service training for NHS staff on drug misuse, to maintain close liaison with the Drugs Training Project at Stirling University and the Scottish Health Education Group, and to seek to work in co-operation with these bodies as appropriate.

5 Scottish Drugs Forum

5.1 In 1986 a new national voluntary organisation, the Scottish Drugs Forum, was established with grant support from SHHD. The forum draws its membership from the voluntary and statutory sectors and its main objective is to undertake a co-ordinating and supporting role for the work of local drugs groups and other individuals and organisations concerned with drugs problems.

SHHD
October 1987

Services for Drug Misusers in Wales

A Paper by the Welsh Office

1 Advice and Counselling

Most areas in Wales have advisory and counselling services and many involve the voluntary sector. They include drop-in centres and peripatetic health professional staff offering a response to both casual enquiries and specific case-related problems. The All Wales Drugline launched in August

99

1986, is a 24 hour manned telephone service. Funded by the Department, it provides immediate advice and guidance to drug misusers, their families, friends and to professional carers. Callers are also advised to seek follow up support from their local services.

2 Treatment and Rehabilitation

Specialist treatment and rehabilitation services for drug misusers are limited in Wales. Apart from statutory provision, two voluntary organisations: Teen Challenge, funded by urban aid, and the Rhoserchan Project, both in Dyfed, offer residential treatment and rehabilitation. The Welsh Committee on Drug Misuse (WCDM) is currently examining the extent of services throughout Wales and is shortly to produce recommendations for action.

3 County services

3.1 Clwyd: Community workers and psychiatric nurses form a community-based counselling and advisory service from two main centres. They work with voluntary councils and statutory agencies including general practitioners and hospital staff. There is a drug treatment unit at the North Wales Hospital. The authority is planning the employment of a counsellor specifically for AIDS and drugs misuse.

3.2 Dyfed: The health authority is developing a pilot multi-disciplinary team. At present only the project leader is in post working with a counsellor from the local voluntary council on alcoholism and drugs. The intention is to provide an advisory and counselling service based at a drop-in centre supported by a consultant psychiatrist, local GPs and members of the local mental health team. Detoxification occurs at general and psychiatric hospitals. In the county there are two residential treatment and rehabilitation centres operated by voluntary agencies – Teen Challenge and the Rhoserchan Project.

3.3 Gwent: The service in Gwent revolves around the health authority's HARP Project. It is an advisory and counselling walk-in centre where information, counselling and development workers operate. Linked to it is a Development Officer in the voluntary sector working with self-help groups. In-patient and out-patient treatment is available from the general psychiatric services.

3.4 Gwynedd: The Gwynedd Drug Advisory Service provides information, advice and counselling. This is staffed by community workers who work closely with trained voluntary counsellors. Consultations are available at psychiatric out-patient clinics. Misusers are generally referred to a consultant psychiatrist who specialises in substance abuse. The Drug Treatment Unit at the North Wales Hospital, Clwyd, also admits patients from Gwynedd.

3.5 Mid Glamorgan: Currently counselling services are provided by the voluntary sector. The health authority is planning a community drug team consisting of a psychiatrist, psychologist, community psychiatric nurse and social worker. Counselling drug misusers about AIDS is also to be a part of the team's work.

3.6 Powys: There are plans for employing an officer to co-ordinate training of volunteer counsellors throughout the county. There is no existing specialist service for drug misusers.

3.7 South Glamorgan: The principal focus for health care for drug misusers is the ADFER, Alcohol and Drug Treatment Unit at a psychiatric hospital. A day care unit has also been established with a community drug team comprising a psychiatrist, psychologist, social worker and nurse. There is specific provision for counselling drug misusers about AIDS. Local voluntary groups also provide information and counselling services.

3.8 West Glamorgan: The main provision of service is in the voluntary sector which offers advice and counselling. There is in-patient and out-patient general psychiatric treatment.

4 Training

Training and the selection of counsellors are considered by many organisations as being of key importance. Drug Advisory committees (DACs) have seen training as an essential element of their strategies for combating drug misuse and this is supported through central funding in a number of counties. The WCDM has issued guidance to DACs on the selection and training of counsellors.

5 Information and Monitoring

DACs have identified considerable problems in collecting reliable information on the incidence and nature of drug misuse. WCDM is introducing two complementary data collection systems. One involves the collection of core data by each DAC on a common basis at six-monthly intervals, for collation nationally. The other is a more in-depth study of problem drug users and their use of services, to be piloted in two counties.

6 Central Funding

6.1 Central funding has contributed significantly to the provisions of core prevention and counselling services in the majority of counties. Further development is planned to make the facilities more comprehensive and particularly to promote developments in treatment and rehabilitation.The Department has allocated £1.64 million since 1985–86 to help statutory authority and voluntary group schemes and bids for funding from 1988–89 are currently being considered. Bids for funding are considered very carefully in the context of county strategies detailing plans for service provision and development, training and co-ordination. These were recently approved by the Secretary of State subject to certain specified improvements being made.

6.2 Recently, the Welsh Office received bids from district health authorities for funds to support AIDS prevention activities and funds (£33,500 p.a.) have been made available specifically for the counselling of drug misusers. Support for further measures is being considered including the provision of clean injecting equipment in the light of the results of pilot schemes in England and Scotland. As a means of monitoring and evaluating the investment, recipients of grant monies have been required to produce thorough progress reports to the Department where they are scrutinised by both administrators and professional staff. To complement the scrutiny officials are to visit a broad selection of these schemes. While funding is on a recurrent basis for the duration of the project, it is subject to review after three years that the service continues to be needed and is effective.

7 Welsh AIDS Campaign

The Welsh AIDS Campaign (WAC) organised a conference and follow up day for drugs fieldworkers on AIDS which was well attended by members from all the principal agencies, both voluntary and statutory. Many agencies now provide information and counselling for drug misusers on AIDS. WAC is seeking to work with these agencies to provide information, educational and training resources on AIDS and drug misuse. They are currently preparing a leaflet for drug misusers on hygienic practices with the advice of WCDM on its content.

Services for Drug Misusers in Northern Ireland

A Paper by the Northern Ireland Office

1 All available statistical information suggests that the overall drugs problem in Northern Ireland is relatively small by comparison with the rest of the United Kingdom. The number of persons charged for offences relating to controlled drugs in 1986 was 317 compared with 286 in 1985. The majority of offences related to cannabis and there is no evidence of any major 'hard drugs' problem, in particular an intravenous injection problem. Evidence from the RUC Drugs Squad indicates that it is very unusual to find individuals in possession of injecting material or equipment in Northern Ireland. The number of addicts notified to the Chief Medical Officer of the Department of Health and Social Services who were still receiving controlled drugs at 31 December 1986 was 11 compared with 13 in 1985. Hospital statistics for 1985, the latest year for which figures are available, show a decrease in admissions for drug-related problems, 101 compared with 135 in 1984, with almost three-quarters of such cases involving non-controlled drugs.

Services

2 Northern Ireland has one regional unit (located in Belfast) which specialises in the treatment of alcohol and drug dependence. In addition facilities for such treatment are available in the six psychiatric hospitals in the Province and in psychiatric units attached to some general hospitals. Each of the six psychiatric hospitals has an identified consultant who specialises in the treatment of addiction. The professional viewpoint in Northern Ireland to date has been that routine maintenance therapy using oral methadone as a substitute for other controlled drugs cannot be regarded as an effective or advisable regime in the management of drug addiction. Aftercare in the community following hospital discharge can be

provided by means of hospital out-patient, day hospital and community support services. Current information indicates that existing services are adequate to cope with the extent of the problem so far identified.

AIDS

3 The incidence of AIDS in Northern Ireland is so far relatively small with three cases identified (all of whom contracted the disease outside the Province and all have since died) plus a further 37 individuals infected with the HIV virus. There have been no cases involving intravenous drug misuse. Screening for HIV antibodies is available from the locations referred to in paragraph 2 and so far all tests have proved negative.

4 Because of the low incidence of injecting drug misuse in the Province the Department of Health and Social Services has decided not to actively promote this element of the Government's national public education campaign in the Province. Facilities at sexually transmitted disease clinics have been enhanced to meet the anticipated increase in demand for HIV testing and counselling. The main voluntary group in Northern Ireland is AIDS Helpline (Northern Ireland) which provides a mainly telephone advice and counselling service. It receives funding from the Department for providing this service.

5 The Department has established a local AIDS Committee to ensure that action to control the spread of infection in the Province is properly co-ordinated and that the public education campaign, whilst continuing to have a largely national focus, is supplemented and adapted as necessary to have maximum impact locally. Because of the potential dangers, the AIDS Committee and the Northern Ireland Committee on Drug Misuse continue to monitor the situation closely.

Implementation in Wales and Northern Ireland

1 Our report, and the conclusions and recommendations in it, apply to the UK as a whole. In this annex we make some brief comments about priorities for implementation in Wales and Northern Ireland.

Wales

2 There is evidence that the extent of injecting drug misuse is quite significant in some parts of Wales but, as yet, prevalence of HIV amongst drug misusers appears to be low. A major opportunity to prevent widespread infection amongst drug misusers therefore exists and must be seized immediately. Community-based services are quite well developed in many parts of Wales and provide a good base for future developments along the lines described in Annex C. Psychiatric back-up for these services appears to be less well developed with only one district having a consultant psychiatrist specialising in this field, and one further specialist planned. Moreover, in a number of areas there is a dearth of doctors who are willing to consider selecting appropriate treatment from the full range of options including prescribing. The availability of sterile needles and syringes in Wales is patchy and there are no official syringe exchange schemes.

3 We see an improvement in psychiatric input, a wider recognition of the value of prescribing in appropriate cases, and measures to increase the availability of injecting equipment, as particular priorities in Wales.

Northern Ireland

4 Although all available statistical information suggests that the prevalence of both drug misuse and HIV infection in Northern Ireland is lower than in other parts of the United Kingdom we feel that it is essential to take every

possible step to ensure that HIV infection is not spread via injecting drug misusers. We therefore consider that the arguments and recommendations in this report are as relevant to Northern Ireland as they are to other parts of the United Kingdom.

5 The number of regular drug injectors in Northern Ireland appears to be fairly small and it may well be that the greater risk of spreading HIV could come from experimental or occasional drug injectors. The development of accessible, community-based services giving harm-reduction advice (as described in Annex C) is therefore particularly important. Such services, combined with outreach work, are likely to be the best way of making contact with experimental or occasional injectors and we therefore see the development of such services as a particular priority for Northern Ireland.

Research References

1 In addition to evidence taken from a number of witnesses, our enquiry also drew upon the available research literature. The following list is not comprehensive, but includes many of the studies which we found valuable.

Des Jarlais, D. C. Stages in the Response of the Drug Abuse Treatment System to the AIDS Epidemic in New York City, in press: Journal of Drug Issues.

Des Jarlais, D. C. and Friedman, S. R. HIV Infection among Intravenous Drug Users: Epidemiology and Risk Reduction, in press: AIDS: an International Bimonthly Journal.

Drucker, E. (1986) AIDS and addiction in New York City. Am J Drug Alcohol Abuse 12(1&2) pp. 165–181.

Glanz, A. (1987) Review of Research Literature on Patterns of Tenure in Treatment of Drug Misusers and Impact on the Behaviour of Drug Misusers of Service Utilisation.

Hartnoll, R. Daviaud, E. and Power, R. (1987) Help-Seeking by Problem Drug Takers: A Review of the Literature, draft.

Parker, H. and Chadwick, C. (1987) Unattractive Alternatives: Dilemmas for Drug Services in Wirral, the fifth report of the Misuse of Drugs Research Project for the Wirral Drug Abuse Committee and the Wirrall District Drug Dependency Problem Team.

Power, R. Daviaud, E. and Hartnoll, R. The effects of AIDS upon Patterns of Injecting and Sharing amongst Regular Drug Users.

Sheehan, M. Oppenheimer, E. and Taylor, C. (1986) Why Drug Users sought help from one London Drug Clinic, British Journal of Addiction 81, 765–775.

WHO Regional Office for Europe. (Copenhagen 1986) AIDS Among Drug Abusers, report on a WHO Consultation.

1987 Presentation to International Conference: Control of Drug Addiction and AIDS in Amsterdam: Services, Experience and Results.

Printed in the United Kingdom for Her Majesty's Stationery Office.
Dd.0290287, 10/89, C30, 3385/4, 5673, 81067.